I0605226

SEVENTEEN

RIGHT HERE RIGHT NOW

Written by Carolyn McHugh

First published in the UK 2025 by Sona Books an imprint of Danann Media Publishing Ltd.

CAT NO: SON0609

Photography courtesy of

Getty images:

Philippe Lopez
Omar Vega
Michael Loccisano
Chung Sung-Jun
THE FACT

The Chosunilbo JNS
Anthony Wallace
Julien De Rosa
Sarah Morris
Gina Wetzler

iMBC
Anna Barclay
Joseph Okpako
Julien Hekimian
Oli Scarff

Anadolu
HLL
Christopher Polk
Frazer Harrison

Other images Alamy, Wiki Commons

Cover design: Darren Grice at Ctrl-d
Book design: Samantha Richiardi at Contradiction Design
Proof reader: Sofia Della Valle

Printed in EU
ISBN: 978-1-917259-07-1

CONTENTS

CONTENTS

KINGS OF K-POP

KINGS OF K-POP

Seventeen performing during their Ode to You tour at the Prudential Center in New Jersey, 2020

BOY GROUP BEHEMOTH SEVENTEEN is one of the most dynamic and influential K-pop groups of our time.

Captivating audiences worldwide with irresistible music, intricate choreography, and unparalleled charm, this 13-member powerhouse has shattered expectations, rising as global Icons through sheer creativity, unity, and relentless hard work.

Although new to Western audiences, Seventeen were the biggest-selling group in the world in 2023 and 2024, and across all artists only Taylor Swift was ahead of them. Yet despite shifting more than 10 million albums worldwide the previous year, the group waited until May 2024 for their first UK Top 40 hit when "Maestro" peaked at #26.

The K-pop sensations have now reached a new level of global fame as their music reaches the UK, Europe, and the US. Their total album sales around the world reached 17 million by the end of 2024, boosted by the phenomenal success of their 10th EP, *FML*, which amassed pre-orders of over 5.2 million copies and went on to sell 6 million copies in South Korea alone. By the end of 2023 it had become the best-selling album in the world.

Their story begins in 2015 when the idols were put together after training with South Korean entertainment company and K-pop specialists Pledis Entertainment.

K-pop, short for Korean pop, is South Korea's unique take on Western pop music—a high-energy fusion of electronic, hip-hop, pop, rock, R&B, and rap. Known for its dynamic style and experimental approach, K-pop often surprises listeners with unexpected twists in its songs.

The genre's roots go back to 11 April 1992, when a hip-hop trio called Seo Taiji and Boys broke onto the scene after appearing on a South Korean talent show. Their fresh approach, combining New Kids on the Block-style boy group charm with bold song topics, resonated deeply with audiences. Their debut song spent 17 weeks at #1, igniting the K-pop phenomenon.

This success aligned with a pivotal shift in South Korea's political landscape, as a more democratic government relaxed its control over music production. Recognising K-pop's export potential, South Korean studios began developing 'idol' groups in the 1990s.

By the 2010s groups such as BTS began to crack the tricky Western markets of the USA, UK, and Europe. In May 2018, their album *Love Yourself; Tear* debuted at #1 on the US Billboard 200 album chart, becoming the first Korean album to top the US album chart and the highest charting album by any Asian act.

Seventeen take the Pyramid Stage during day three of the 2024 Glastonbury Festival, England

Since then several K-pop groups have built on this success – with Seventeen the biggest to date and with the added attribute of being self-producing idols. Their self-produced music, a rarity in the industry, has won praise for its authenticity and innovation. This involvement in the creative process is one of Seventeen's most distinguishing features. As 'self-producing idols', they actively participate in songwriting, choreography, and production. This hands-on approach has not only earned them respect within the industry but also allowed them to maintain a distinct and cohesive artistic identity. Members like Woozi, S.Coups, and Hoshi have been particularly instrumental in shaping the group's sound and vision.

Woozi attends the press conference for the group's 8th mini album, *Your Choice,* at the InterContinental Seoul COEX Harmony Ballroom in Seoul, South Korea, 2021

Woozi explained more about the process in an interview with *People* magazine in 2021, saying, 'When we work on an album, we have a group meeting. We all come together and we establish a working culture and a process where it's a free exchange of ideas and nobody hesitates to express their opinions or throw out their ideas — not just in music, but in all aspects of the album.

'It's a very open process and it really comes naturally. This is something that we've seen since we were very young, first starting out.'

K-POP AND THE IDOL SYSTEM: A COMPETITIVE PIPELINE

K-pop's rise is largely attributed to its rigorous idol training system. Studios recruit trainees, often as young as 11, who undergo years of intense vocal and dance training, often working up to 14-hour days with minimal time off.

Trainees live in academies, where they perfect their craft under relentless schedules. Regular evaluations determine their progress, and only the most polished performers get to make their 'debut'. The process involves reshuffling groups to find the optimal combination of talent, creating a competitive, high-stakes environment akin to a mix of stage school and global talent competitions.

Initially, K-pop dominated Asian markets, particularly Japan, before setting its sights on the West. Cracking the US and UK music scenes—a traditionally elusive market—posed a significant challenge. But, through a mix of polished performances, dedicated fan engagement, and strategic global marketing, K-pop has made remarkable inroads in the West, transforming into a global cultural phenomenon.

In contrast to Western pop groups, which typically consist of three to five members, K-pop groups often feature much larger lineups, with some of the most popular groups boasting double-digit memberships. It's seemingly a case of the more the merrier as these multi-multi-member groups seem to attract fans rather than discourage them. In fact many fans say they find larger groups even more appealing. But the shared spotlight can sometimes blur individual personalities and so to address this, the K-pop industry has introduced smaller 'sub-units' within its groups over the past two decades. Working within a sub-unit allows idols to expand their reach even further and display their diverse talents.

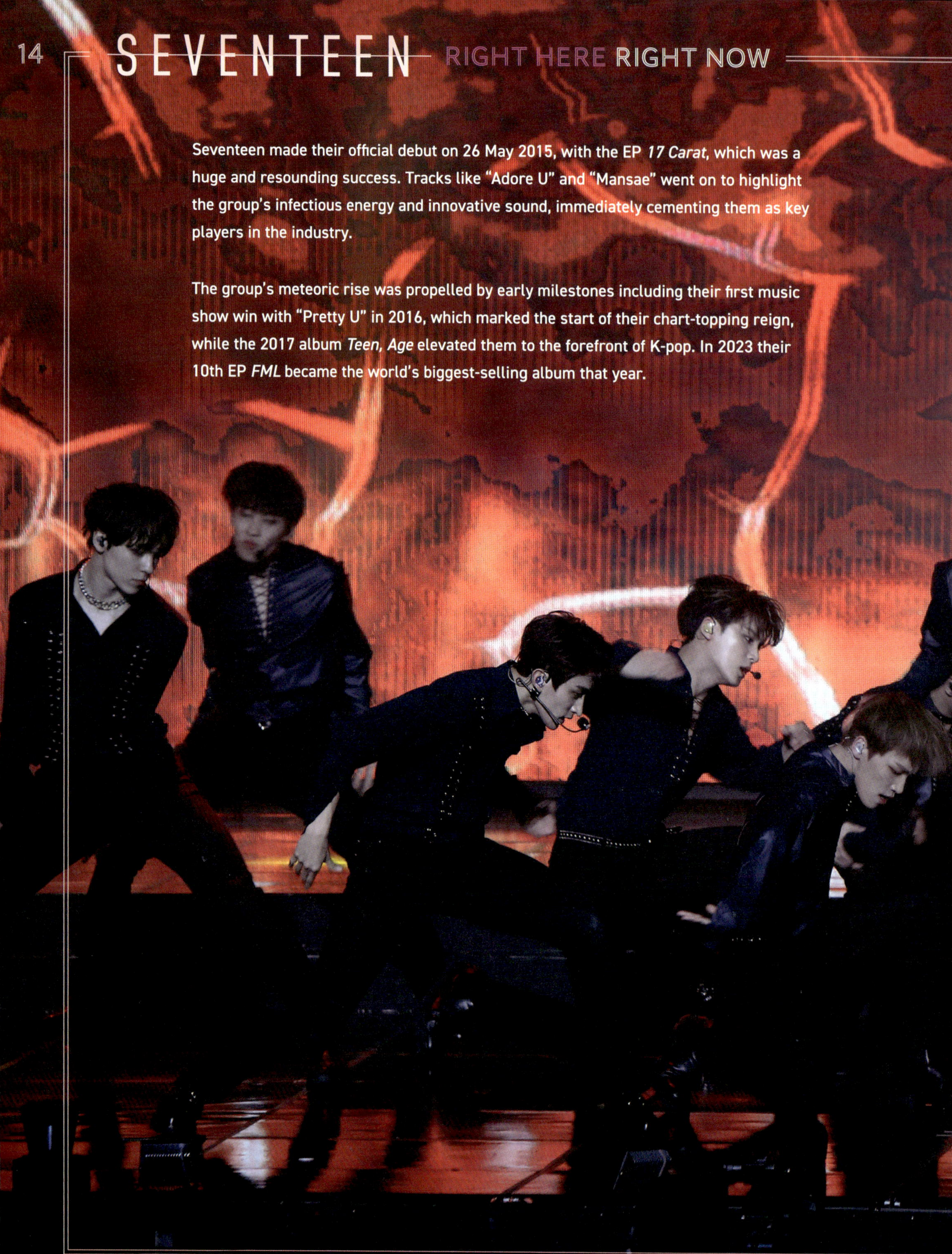

Seventeen made their official debut on 26 May 2015, with the EP *17 Carat*, which was a huge and resounding success. Tracks like "Adore U" and "Mansae" went on to highlight the group's infectious energy and innovative sound, immediately cementing them as key players in the industry.

The group's meteoric rise was propelled by early milestones including their first music show win with "Pretty U" in 2016, which marked the start of their chart-topping reign, while the 2017 album *Teen, Age* elevated them to the forefront of K-pop. In 2023 their 10th EP *FML* became the world's biggest-selling album that year.

The group's charismatic stage presence, elevated by meticulous attention to detail and synchronised choreography, has become their hallmark.

Seventeen's influence now extends far beyond South Korea as their global tours, sold-out concerts, and international fan meets prove. They have successfully penetrated markets in Asia, North America, and Europe, bridging cultural gaps with their music. Their 2019 world tour, Ode to You, confirmed their status as global superstars, with performances in major cities across multiple continents. This is their story so far ...

Seventeen perform on stage at the 8th Gaon Chart K-Pop Awards on January 23, 2019, in Seoul, South Korea

MEET THE GROUP

MEET THE GROUP

THE LUCKY THIRTEEN who make up the group are, in alphabetical order, Dino, DK, Hoshi, Jeonghan, Joshua, Jun, Mingyu, S. Coups, Seungkwan, The8, Vernon, Wonwoo and Woozi. Together they get their name, Seventeen, from having 13 members, divided into three units, to make one group. To do the maths this means 13 members + three units + 1 group = Seventeen. Of course these multi-talented Seventeen idols can do it all, but each unit has their own specialty.

Seventeen attend the press conference for the group's compilation album, *17 Is Right Here*, at Conrad Seoul in Yeongdeungpo-gu in Seoul, South Korea, April 2024

The three units working within the group are hip-hop, vocals and performance. Seventeen is celebrated as being 'self-producing' with members like Woozi, S.Coups, and Hoshi playing pivotal roles in songwriting, choreography, and production. This creative autonomy gives their work a unique authenticity and cohesion that resonates deeply with fans and critics alike.

STRENGTH IN NUMBERS
STRENGTH IN NUMBERS

EACH GROUP MEMBER IS PART OF A UNIT WITHIN THE WHOLE GROUP, AS FOLLOWS:

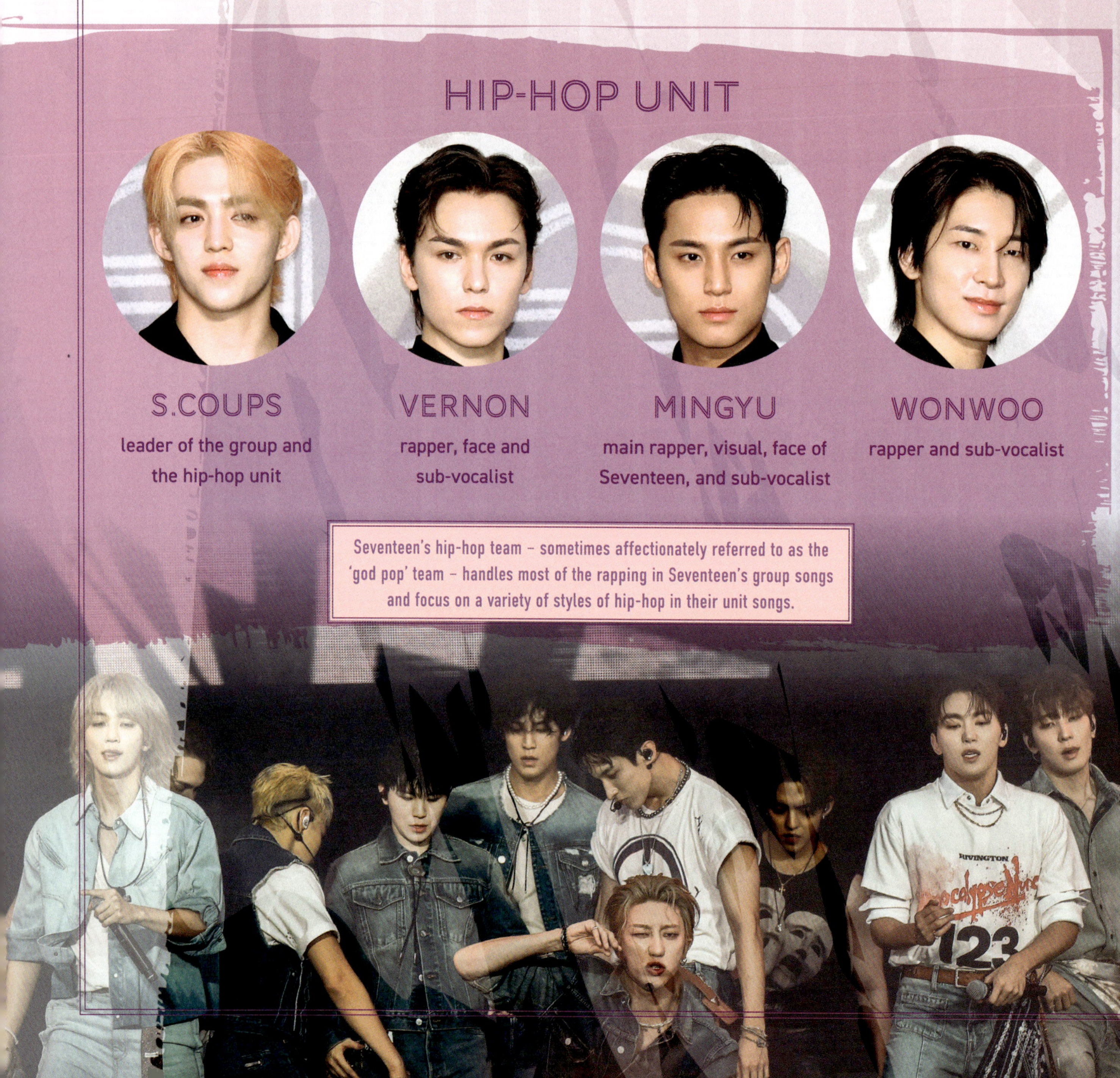

HIP-HOP UNIT

S.COUPS
leader of the group and the hip-hop unit

VERNON
rapper, face and sub-vocalist

MINGYU
main rapper, visual, face of Seventeen, and sub-vocalist

WONWOO
rapper and sub-vocalist

Seventeen's hip-hop team – sometimes affectionately referred to as the 'god pop' team – handles most of the rapping in Seventeen's group songs and focus on a variety of styles of hip-hop in their unit songs.

VOCAL UNIT

WOOZI
leader of the vocal unit (songwriter and producer)

SEUNGKWAN
vocalist

JEONGHAN
vocalist

JOSHUA
vocalist

DK
vocalist

The vocal team can sing it all and their powerful harmonies provide backing vocals that inject emotional depth into all Seventeen songs.

PERFORMANCE UNIT

HOSHI
leader of the performance unit (choreography)

JUN
dancer and sub-vocalist

THE8
dancer and sub-vocalist

DINO
dancer, sub-vocalist, and maknae

While performance is often used as shorthand for dance, Seventeen's performance team takes a more holistic approach to performance, seeing it instead as an artform that combines everything from dance to singing, rapping, and posing.

DINO

BORN: 11 FEBRUARY 1999 (AQUARIUS)
HEIGHT: 5FT 8INS

BIRTH NAME LEE CHAN, Dino is the youngest member of Seventeen, a position known as 'maknae'. After graduating from Seoul Broadcasting High School in 2017, he underwent a rigorous idol training process, specialising in dance and choreography. He made his debut with Seventeen as the group's main dancer within the Performance team.

He has since showcased his choreographic talents by creating routines for several tracks, including "Jam Jam" and "Flower", and in 2023 he released his first solo tape "Wait". His other musical projects include contributing to the original soundtrack for the Korean web drama *A-Teen* in 2018. This streamed series of 24 eight-minute episodes, about six high school students and how they deal with their teenage years, was a huge hit in the group's homeland where it attracted a cumulative 200 million views for its first season and 300 million for its second.

As well as being one of the group's key dancers, Dino, as the maknae of Seventeen, carries the unique role of being the youngest member who not only brings vibrant energy and charm but continuously supports his fellow members, strengthening the group's bond.

Instagram: @feat.dino

Dino performs live on stage at the UNESCO headquarters in Paris, France, in November, 2023

DK performs at the 39th Golden Disc Awards at Mizuho PayPay Dome in Fukuoka, Japan, in January 2025

DK

BORN: 18 FEBRUARY 1997 (AQUARIUS)

HEIGHT: 5FT 11INS

DK, SHORT FOR DOKYEOM, was born Lee Seokmin in South Korea. He is among Seventeen's strongest vocalists, as well as leading the special sub-unit 'BSS' (BooSeokSoon), alongside Hoshi and Seungkwan. His full stage name, Dokyeom, indicates his desire to be a multi-talented artist, with 'Do' meaning 'many' and 'Kyeom' meaning 'talents'.

Outside of his work with Seventeen, he is also a talented musical theatre performer and took the lead role of King Arthur in the lavish, Broadway-style Korean musical *XCalibur* in 2019, backed by a 75-strong cast and a 28-piece orchestra.

Instagram: @dk_is_dokyeom

HOSHI

BORN: 15 JUNE 1996 (GEMINI)
HEIGHT: 5FT 10INS

LEADER OF THE PERFORMANCE UNIT, Hoshi is renowned as an exceptional dancer and choreographer. He was first inspired to dance after learning the martial art of Taekwondo – he is a black belt – and found the poses were similar to dancing. Hoshi is also a member of the special sub-teams BSS and SVT Leaders.

The stage name 'Hoshi' is an abbreviation for 'Horangi-ui Siseon', meaning 'tiger's gaze' in Korean, signifying his focus and determination. He builds on this persona by frequently wearing tiger-themed outfits with dazzling stage entrances that are fast becoming legendary. Strutting around in striking ensembles, he electrifies the crowd as fans respond with their own tiger-claw hand gestures in acknowledgement. His favourite pose is his signature 'Horanghae' stance. Horanghae is a word Hoshi invented by combining the Korean words for tiger (horangi) and I love you (saranghae) to make 'I tiger you'. It's said to mean that he's telling fans he loves them in his own language.

Primarily responsible for creating and directing the group's choreography, Hoshi has brought to life some of Seventeen's most dynamic and memorable dance numbers. Among his credits are dance routines for hit songs including *Don't Wanna Cry*, *Clap*, and *Very Nice*, where his innovative choreography blends storytelling with precision. Hoshi also makes a significant contribution to the group's vocal performances, and went on to release his first solo mixtape, *Spider*, produced with Woozi in April 2021.

Hoshi is a proficient Japanese speaker, which enhances the group's engagement with Japanese fans and the broader Japanese music market.

Instagram: @ho5hi_kwon

Hoshi live on stage at the 39th Golden Disc Awards at Mizuho PayPay Dome in Fukuoka, Japan, in January 2025

JEONGHAN

BORN: 4 OCTOBER 1995 (LIBRA)
HEIGHT: 5FT 10INS

A KEY MEMBER OF THE VOCAL TEAM, Jeonghan is also recognised for his stage charisma, dance skills and ability to connect with audiences. Most recently he teamed up with Wonwoo to form Seventeen's third sub-unit, Jeonghan X Wonwoo (JxW) which had a big hit with its first single album *This Man*.

He is affectionately nicknamed 'Angel' by fans because his birthday dates sound like the word angel in Korean and the caring aspect of his personality has earned him the role of the group's mother figure, known for checking on the wellbeing of his groupmates.

Early in Seventeen's career, Jeonghan became famous for his signature long, flowing hair, which he has styled in all sorts of looks. In 2024, he was proudly appointed as an ambassador of the luxury brand Acqua di Parma.

Instagram: @jeonghaniyoo_n

Jeonghan on stage during the Glastonbury Festival in England, 2024

JOSHUA

BORN: 30 DECEMBER 1995 (CAPRICORN)
HEIGHT: 5FT 10INS

JOSHUA HONG WAS BORN and raised in Los Angeles, USA, before moving to South Korea in 2013 when he had finished high school to pursue a career in music. He is part of the group's vocal unit.

Speaking in his home city when Seventeen stopped off to perform two sell-out shows at the BMO Stadium at the end of their American tour, Joshua highlighted the similarities between his group and his hometown.

'We both thrive on the endless possibilities that diversity creates,' he said. 'LA stands tall as capital of culture and creativity, fuelled by bustling energy created by people from diverse backgrounds. Seventeen is like that too. The 13 of us have come together with our different personalities and tastes to create a kind of dynamic and creative spirit that's unique to Seventeen.'

While in LA, Seventeen was presented with a certificate of appreciation from the City of Los Angeles for its contributions to music and youth empowerment for through the "Seventeen the City Los Angeles" project, which involved decorating downtown LA and its iconic landmarks with Seventeen-themed colours and displays.

Instagram: @joshu_acoustic

Joshua performs at the 39th Golden Disc Awards at Mizuho PayPay Dome in Fukuoka, Japan, in January 2025

JUN

BORN: 10 JUNE 1996 (GEMINI)
HEIGHT: 6FT

JUN, BORN WEN JUNHUI in Shenzhen, China, is a key figure in the group's performance team, serving as a lead dancer and sub-vocalist.

Before his debut with the group, Jun was an established child actor in China, appearing in various films and television series. This acting background contributes to his expressive performances on stage.

Jun has since showcased his talents with solo singles, including 2018's "Can You Sit By My Side?"

Along with his fellow Chinese groupmate The8, Jun plays a significant role in bridging cultural connections between Korean and Chinese fans, enhancing the group's international appeal.

Instagram: @junhui_moon

Jun performs live on stage during the Glastonbury Festival in England, 2024

Sub-units are common in the K-pop industry where they have become a trademark strategy for showcasing the talents and personalities of group members. As the name suggests, they comprise a small group formed from the larger core group of idols, which will have separate music releases and usually different concepts to show group members working in genres and performance styles not typically explored by the larger group.

Seventeen have three special sub-units, BSS, SVT Leaders and Jeonghan X Wonwoo (JxW).

BSS, (BooSeokSoon) comprising DK (its leader), Hoshi, and Seungkwan, debuted on 21 March 2018 with the single "Just Do It". There was then a five year hiatus before the release of their second single *"Second Wind"*.

SVT Leaders is a trio consisting of the leaders of Seventeen's sub-units, Hoshi, S.Coups and Woozi.

Jeonghan X Wonwoo (JxW) This duo is Seventeen's newest sub-unit, comprising Jeonghan and Wonwoo, which debuted mid-2024 with immediate commercial success.

MINGYU

BORN: 6 APRIL 1997 (ARIES)
HEIGHT: 6FT 2INS

LEAD RAPPER in the hip-hop unit, Mingyu, born Kim Min Gyu in South Korea, is not only at the top of his rap game but also one of the group's lead visuals.

His involvement can be heard particularly in tracks like "Adore U", "Mansae", and "Pretty U", which he refers to as part of a narrative trilogy.

Among the most fashion-forward members of Seventeen, Mingyu was named an ambassador for French luxury fashion house Dior in August 2024. Later that year, he also took center stage in a high-profile Calvin Klein campaign for a denim collection in autumn.

Creative in his own right, Mingyu has designed some of the group's merchandise, including the 'Bongbongie,' the group's official light stick. Beyond music, Mingyu's interests include sports, especially football and basketball.

Instagram: @min9yu_k

Mingyu live on stage during the Glastonbury Festival in England, 2024

S.Coups performs on stage during the Glastonbury Festival in England, 2024

S.COUPS

BORN: 8 AUGUST 1995 (LEO)
HEIGHT: 5FT 10INS

AS THE GENERAL LEADER, S.Coups oversees the group activities and cohesion, while also heading up the hip-hop sub-units and guiding its rap performances and compositions. He is also leader of the special sub-unit SVT Leaders, alongside other team leaders Hoshi and Woozi.

He has been instrumental in Seventeen's musical direction, contributing as a rapper, lyricist, and composer. Notable works include the group's debut EP *17 Carat* (2015) and albums *Love & Letter* (2016) *Teen, Age* (2017) *An Ode* (2019) and *Face the Sun* (2022). While notable tracks include "Adore U", "Mansae", "Clap", "Fear", and "Left & Right".

The Y! entertainment site has described him as the group's 'confident and thoroughly captivating anchor' and he is certainly a pivotal figure in Seventeen's success. So there was understandable concern when he took a hiatus for health reasons in late 2019, followed by much rejoicing when he came back to work in 2020.

Instagram: @sound_of_coups

SEUNGKWAN

BORN: 16 JANUARY 1998 (CAPRICORN)
HEIGHT: 5FT 9INS

SINGER/SONGWRITER AND ONE of Seventeen's strongest vocalists, Seungkwan is also in the group's successful sub-unit BSS, with Hoshi and DK.

Known for his energetic performances, powerful vocals and engaging personality, Seungkwan's contributions to the group's discography include vocals on "Adore U", "Mansae", "Pretty U", "Don't Wanna Cry" and "Clap".

Outside of the group he has written the original soundtracks for Korean dramas, including "Kind of Love" (for *Mother* in 2018), "Go" (for *Record of Youth* in 2020), and "The Reason" (for *Lovestruck in the City*).

He took a health-related hiatus from the group in July 2023, returning to work in September ahead of the release of the *Seventeenth Heaven* album.

In November 2024, he was proudly appointed the role of honorary ambassador for Jeju Island, his hometown in South Korea.

Instagram: @pledis_boos

Seungkwan performs on stage during the Glastonbury Festival in England, 2024

THE8

BORN: 7 NOVEMBER 1997 (SCORPIO)
HEIGHT: 5FT 11INS

LEAD DANCER THE8 **practiced Chinese Wushu (martial arts) from the age of five and was also a 'b-boy' (break dancing specialist) in China for six years before joining Pledis Entertainment as a trainee. Now lead dancer, sub vocalist and sub rapper for Seventeen, his skill in b-boying and the associated rhythmic and acrobatic movements have made him invaluable in the group's dance performances and as a choreographer.**

Alongside his work on the group's albums since 2015, The8's solo releases include the singles "Dreams Come True" in 2019, "Falling Down" in 2020 and "Side By Side" in 2021. In 2024, he released *Stardust*, his first EP.

As one of the Chinese members of Seventeen (his birth name is Xu Minghao), he bridges cultures by bringing Chinese elements into the group's performances and promoting cross-cultural appreciation.

Instagram: @xuminghao_o

The8 performs live on stage at the Lollapalooza Festival held at the Olympiastadion, Berlin, in September 2024

VERNON

BORN: 18 FEBRUARY 1998 (AQUARIUS)
HEIGHT: 5FT 10INS

BORN HANSOL VERNON CHWE, in New York, USA, Vernon is a Korean American rapper and songwriter, who moved to South Korea with his Korean mother and American father when he was five years old.

As one of Seventeen's main rappers and a sub-vocalist, he is key to the group's rap sections and overall musical direction. He has songwriting credits on over 90 songs, making him the group member with the second-most writing credits after Woozi. Together with Woozi and Dino, he also contributed to the soundtrack of the hit web drama *A-Teen*, which attracted 300 million viewers.

His solo releases include "Bands Boy" in 2021 and "Black Eye" in 2022. He also featured on Charli XCX's remix of "Beg for You" in 2022.

Instagram: @vernonline

Vernon live on stage at the 39th Golden Disc Awards at Mizuho PayPay Dome in Fukuoka, Japan, in January 2025

WONWOO

BORN: 17 JULY 1996 (CANCER)
HEIGHT: 6FT

BORN IN SOUTH KOREA, rapper/singer/songwriter Wonwoo is also a member of Seventeen's third sub-unit, Jeonghan X Wonwoo (JxW) which debuted on 17 June 2024 with their first single album *This Man*. This debut album achieved significant commercial success, breaking the first-week sales record for a K-pop sub-unit album within four days of its release.

As part of Seventeen's hip-hop team, he has contributed to over 35 songs.

Outside of the group, Wonwoo featured in Dive Studio's *Mindset* series in 2023, releasing episodes detailing his relationship with mental health, and offering insights and support to fans.

Instagram: @everyone_woo

Wonwoo attends the press conference for the group's album, *17 Is Right Here*, at the Conrad Seoul in Seoul, South Korea, 2024

WOOZI

BORN: 22 NOVEMBER 1996 (SCORPIO/SAGITTARIUS CUSP)

HEIGHT: 5FT 5INS

LEADER OF SEVENTEEN'S vocal team, and the group's principal composer and producer, singer/songwriter Woozi is also part of the sub-unit 'SVT Leaders'. He was born in South Korea as Lee Ji-hoon and is an only child. He studied classical music from an early age and learned to play the clarinet, among other instruments.

Frequently described as a 'genius composer', Woozi writes for other artists outside of Seventeen. Along with Vernon and Dino he worked on the soundtrack for the Korean web drama sensation *A-Teen.*

But one of his biggest successes came with fellow Seventeen group member Hoshi, when the pair had a hit with the song "Spider" which debuted at #5 on the Billboard World Digital Song Sales chart in April 2021. In that same year he picked up the Best Producer prize at the 6th Asia Artist Awards, becoming the youngest ever winner in history.

He then released some solo work – his first one-track mixtape *Ruby* on 3 January 2022 – written in English it topped the charts in 18 different regions, including Chile, Mexico, and Indonesia.

'To be honest, [writing the song in English] wasn't easy,' Woozi told *Teen Vogue* in a 2022 interview. 'I thought a lot about what language would fit the song best. At first, I wasn't thinking about English per se. But as I began writing the song, I just thought that English was very intuitive, very cool. When I thought about a language that could incorporate the colour of the song fully, that was English. So although it was challenging, I thought it was very appropriate. And I got a lot of help from my colleagues, which was really great.'

Instagram: @woozi_universefactory

Woozi performs with the group during the Glastonbury Festival in England, June, 2024

A DAZZING DEBUT
A DAZZLING DEBUT

BEFORE THEIR OFFICIAL DEBUT, the members of Seventeen underwent an extensive and gruelling training period, common to the K-pop industry. The training process is tough, with the emphasis on discipline, repetition, and perfection. It is a very demanding regime and many wannabe idols simply don't make the grade.

The members of Seventeen posing at their *Seventeen Project: Debut Big Plan* showcase, broadcast in May, 2015

The boys of Seventeen were first introduced to the public on the Ustream reality show *Seventeen TV*, which showed all the contestants training and hoping to make it into the group.

Originally there were to have been 17 group members, but in the end only 13 contestants made the cut. (The four former pre-debut trainees who left the process were Jang Do-yoon, Samuel Kim, Shin Dong-jin and Yao Mingming.

But the name Seventeen was retained as it still worked – with some maths!
13 musicians + 3 units (vocals, hip-hop, and performance specialists) + 1 group
= Seventeen.

A reality show, called *Seventeen Project: Debut Big Plan*, documented the final stages of their preparation, providing fans with an intimate look at the rigorous process that K-pop idols endure. This rarely seen, behind-the-scenes exposure not only highlighted their dedication and resilience but also helped to foster a deep connection with their burgeoning fanbase.

The successful final 13 members were introduced to the public during their official debut on 26 May 2015, a one-hour live showcase which was broadcast on MBC, South Korea's main terrestrial tv channel. It was also broadcast on Naver's V App.

The group began picking up fans almost before it was born as the auditions for its members were screened in a live-streamed online show called Seventeen TV. Unscripted and unedited, the show gave viewers a chance to see everything that went on during the gruelling rounds of training including the brutally honest process of evaluations as each trainee is rated. The streaming also showed some sweet moments outside their professional work, as group members got to know each other, ate meals and played around. There is even footage online of a time when they all stand silently while being told off for not working hard enough.

At one point the series came off air for months and when it reappeared the existing line up had been finalised as a few of the original members were nowhere to be seen.

The group's eventual debut was on Munhwa Broadcasting Corporation (MBC) - one of South Korea's main public broadcasters which has played a significant role in the Korean Wave (Hallyu), promoting Korean culture, entertainment, and media globally.

Members of the South Korean band pose on the red carpet of the 2015 Mnet Asian Music Awards in Hong Kong on December 2, 2015

Following their official performance debut, Seventeen were ready to release their first EP. And They did it in glittering style.

The five-track EP, *17 Carat*, was released on 29 May 2015 and immediately marked them out as one of the most promising rookie groups of the year. It was a bold introduction to their musical identity, versatility, and talent.

17 Carat's musically diverse five tracks impressed critics, who also felt that the group's impressive self-production capabilities set them apart from most other idol groups. The members' involvement in the production process, with Woozi taking a central role in songwriting and composing, added an authentic and personal touch to their music. This hands-on approach to their craft would become a defining characteristic of Seventeen, earning them the title of 'self-producing idols'.

Despite the group's relative youth and inexperience, their sound was polished, mature, fresh, and energetic.

The lead single, "Adore U", was an upbeat, catchy track that highlighted their harmonious vocals and intricate choreography. The song's infectious melody and youthful energy quickly caught the attention of K-pop fans both domestically and internationally, where the song went on to perform strongly, in both markets.

In South Korea, where the EP has sold over 82,972 copies, it peaked at # 4 on the Gaon Album Chart.

In America it made #8 on the US Billboard World Albums Chart and stayed on the chart for 11 weeks - a rare feat for a rookie group - and *Billboard* named *17 Carat* as the 'Best K-pop Album of 2015'.

Track list

Shining Diamond

An anthemic, upbeat track that serves as an introduction to the group's energy and charm.

Adore U

The lead single, a catchy and playful song that is a genre-swirling gem.

Ah Yeah

A dynamic and powerful track featuring the group's performance unit, displaying their dance skills and stage presence.

Jam Jam

A fun and funky song that emphasises Seventeen's vocal harmonies and playful lyrics.

20

A mellow and introspective track that reveals a more mature and reflective side of the group.

The group stated that the track list was chosen to reflect their core concept of 'boys' passion'. The album had two physical versions: one black and one white themed photo card set.

All copies include a CD containing the songs and a fold-up poster/lyric sheet.

Dino and Hoshi at a fansign in Yongsan-gu, October 18, 2015

Seventeen actively promoted 17 Carat through various music shows and live performances. The group's live performances of "Adore U" were particularly praised for their intricate choreography and synchronisation, which has gone on to become a signature aspect of Seventeen's appeal.

The group's tireless promotion and engaging performances played a crucial role in their rapid rise to fame. Their ability to connect with fans through energetic and polished live shows helped to solidify their reputation as one of the most talented and hardworking rookie groups of their time. Their innovative use of a unit system, dividing the members into Hip-Hop, Vocal, and Performance sub-units, allowed them to highlight individual strengths while maintaining a cohesive group dynamic. This structure provided a unique viewing experience, making their performances more engaging and diverse.

Social media platforms buzzed with fan-made content, from dance covers to reaction videos, further amplifying their presence in the K-pop community.

Ending 2015 as the most impressive male rookie group of the year, Seventeen had given due notice that they would be a formidable presence in the K-pop industry. And their first performances of "Adore U" particularly proved they weren't going to let the spotlight slip. Hoshi pretending to give CPR to S.Coups, forming a human train, and pretending to be a train on stage all demonstrated how their bursts of unpredictable, playful choreography was perfectly designed to entertain—and to be unforgettable.

Adore U

The EP's lead single "Adore U" was an absolutely stand-out track. Insanely catchy, it was written by Seventeen's Woozi and S. Coups, together with Yeon Dong-geon, a South Korean actor, hip-hop recording artist, record producer, and breakdancer. It is the first in a trilogy of singles (followed by "Mansae", and "Pretty U") about a boy and girl meeting and falling in love – once the boy had cracked the age-old difficulty of summoning up the courage to ask the girl out.

It sold more than 38,000 digital copies and peaked at # 13 on the Billboard US World Chart.

Seventeen perform at the 2015 Summer K-POP Festival on August 4, 2015, held at Seoul Plaza, South Korea

In the context of K-pop, the term 'rookie' refers to a newly debuted artist or group who is in the early stage of their career. Rookies are typically within their first year or two of entering the music industry and are still establishing their presence and fan base. Rookies are closely watched by both fans and industry professionals to gauge their potential and future success.

RO

In September 2015, the group released their second mini-album, *Boys Be*. This mix of ballads and dancefloor smash hits made history by getting to #1on the US Billboard World Chart. It sold 170,000 copies in Korea alone and went on to become the highest-selling rookie album of the year.

The title track, "Mansae", became a big hit, earning them widespread attention and multiple rookie awards including Best New Artist at the MAMA Awards and the Golden Disc Awards.

These early successes were about more than numbers and chart positions; they represented the beginning of a journey that would see Seventeen evolve into one of K-pop's most beloved groups. Their debut demonstrated that with talent, dedication, and a genuine connection with fans, even the loftiest dreams could be realised.

Seventeen on stage at the 2015 Summer K-POP Festival on August 4, 2015, held at Seoul Plaza, South Korea

TIMELINE
10 YEARS AT THE TOP

AFTER SEVENTEEN'S SUCCESSFUL DEBUT with the *17 Carat* album, the group quickly rose to prominence within the K-pop industry and began solidifying their reputation as self-producing idols. Here's a year-by-year breakdown of what followed their initial success.

Seventeen holds a showcase for their 3rd mini album *Going Seventeen* in Seoul, South Korea, in December, 2016

2016

FIRST FULL-LENGTH ALBUM AND BREAKTHROUGH

The group's first full-length studio album, *Love & Letter* was released in April 2016, featuring the title track "Pretty U" and "Very Nice", a track which would become a mainstay of their live shows. The album highlighted their ability to blend catchy melodies with intricate choreography, further cementing their identity.

Love & Letter topped the charts in Korea, made #8 in Japan and also entered the Billboard World Albums Chart, which ranks the most popular world music albums in the US.

Seventeen also began gaining traction on the Billboard Social 50 Chart, which tracks the most active artists on social media platforms including Twitter, YouTube, and Facebook, demonstrating their increasing global presence and fan engagement.

The group then embarked on its first concert tour Shining Diamonds, completing 17 shows between July and September in South Korea, Japan, Singapore, Indonesia, Australia, and China.

Most importantly they launched their official fan club and its name. As S.Coups put it when he announced the news to fans on 14 February 2016, 'You always make us shine so bright, so you guys are now going to be our CARAT!'

The name comes from the measuring unit used to grade diamonds and also references the name of their debut record *17 Carat* and its lead track "Shining Diamonds".

GLOBAL EXPANSION

Seventeen performed their first American concerts as part of their 17-date Diamond Edge world tour, visiting 13 cities across the US and Asia.

Added to the set list were tracks from their third EP *Going Seventeen* including the hit track "BoomBoom", and their fourth EP *Al1* (pronounced 'alone'), with its broody electropop hit "Don't Wanna Cry". The music video for "Don't Wanna Cry" clocked up 200 million views on YouTube, the first of Seventeen's videos to do so.

Both albums performed exceptionally well on the Gaon and Billboard charts.

Their second album *Teen, Age* (pronounced with a pause between the two words) plus the single "Clap", did well in the US, Japan and domestically in South Korea.

Seventeen live on stage during a showcase for the group's second album *Teen, Age* in Seoul in November, 2017

GOING SEVENTEEN WEB SERIES

Going Seventeen is also the name of Seventeen's official web variety series, featuring the group members in a mix of comedy, reality, and game-show formats. Launched in 2017, the show has evolved into a fan-favourite known for its comedy skits, chaotic energy, and creative concepts and ranks among the most watched K-pop idol web series on YouTube.

Originally focused mainly on behind-the-scenes content and travel vlogs, the series has shifted over the years to a structured variety show format, including games, missions, pranks, escape rooms, and role-playing scenarios. Popular features include **Mafia Games**, where members play intense psychological deduction games, **Ego Room** where the group confronts past embarrassing moments, **Don't Lie** –which is a muder-mafia style mafia game that has become a big fan-favourite and **Ad-Lib** that uses improvisation to create an acting challenge.

Seventeen perform to showcase their fourth mini album *Al1* at an event at Olympic Hall, Olympic Park, in Seoul on May 23, 2017

2018-2019

ARTISTIC GROWTH AND INTERNATIONAL STARDOM

2018 saw the release of the EPs *You Make My Day* and *You Made My Dawn*. Hit tracks hits like "Oh My!" and "Home" - the latter in a style of music influenced by dubstep and trap - showed the group expanding its range and winning multiple awards. *You Make My Day* went to #1 in Korea with its 500,000 sales earning platinum certification.

Then in 2019 came the album *An Ode*, their third studio full album, which had a darker and more experimental tone than their earlier work and included the tracks "Hit" and "Fear". A big hit, the album won Album of the Year at the Asia Artist Awards and helped the group make its first inroads into European markets, particularly France and Poland. Critics and reviewers praised the album's maturity and artistic ambition. Seoulbeats, the online site specialising in South Korean music and entertainment, described it as, '...a carefully organised and delivered album that shows maturity, personality and a desire to be seen as art.' A fan praised it as being, 'peak K-pop EDM'.

But the biggest accolade of all came when the team at *Billboard* in the US selected *An Ode* as the best K-pop album of the year, from a batch of albums they described as 'amazing'.

'*An Ode* is a pristinely-produced 11-track LP that spends its time showcasing the group's distinct artistry while showing that they haven't left their youthful, playful past behind wholly but have grown into their own sonically', said the *Billboard* review.

'Beginning with the promise of sharing their rambunctious "Hit" sound with the world in the straight up banger of an opening track, the poetic nature of *An Ode* begins with the melodious "Lie Again", which leads to the drama of the introspective lead single "Fear". "Let Me Hear You Say" with its rollicking take on Seventeen's brand of playful electronic dance tracks follows and opens up the album to its central section, leading into the section where smaller units of members get to show off their musical flair.

'Throughout it all, *An Ode* may be aimed at listeners but it is truly an homage to Seventeen's thoughts and artistry and showed us all how to remain earnest to an identity while still evolving. And it's an instant K-pop classic because of it.'

The album's success, coupled with the band having made its official debut in Japan, further extended their reach. Their second world tour, Ode to You which included dates in North America and Europe as well as Asia, drew huge crowds, including a Mexican show which netted over US$750,000. But the final leg was cancelled – including all the European dates – because of the restrictions brought in around the Covid-19 global pandemic. The YouTube documentary series *Hit the Road* gives a great behind-the-scenes view of the tour.

The band performs on stage during the 8th Gaon Chart K-Pop Awards on January 23, 2019 in Seoul, South Korea

2020
SUPERSTARS

In June 2020, the group released the EP which would make them superstars, *Heng:garæ,* which sold over a million copies within days of its release – making it the group's first million-seller. It topped the Japanese charts and crucially the iTunes albums chart in 27 countries. Two singles from the six-track mini-album, "My My" and "Left & Right" were outright exuberant dance floor fillers. Overall the album had a more energetic and fun vibe than the tracks such as "Hit" and "Fear" from its more intense predecessor.

Seventeen built on this breakthough by releasing the six-track EP *: [Semicolon]* in October. This EP, also known as, a 'special album', amassed pre-sales of a million copies. New songs included elements of funk, acid jazz and bossa nova and explored themes of encouragement and comfort – well timed as this was all at the height of the Covid-19 pandemic. Consequently, the album's promotion was limited, with the group making just a few socially distanced television performances. Despite this obstacle, the lead single, "Home;Run", an up-tempo swing and dance-pop song with strong brass and jazz-inflected piano elements, became huge, with its official music video amassing some 34 million views in October 2020. As of January 2025, the video had accumulated over 80 million views.

The track's success was boosted by an appearance on the hit US television show *The Late Late Show with James Corden*. The group began their performance by entering the studio dressed in black t-shirts marked with the show's logo, posing as 'crew', and clearing up with mops and brooms before joining together, changing into sparkly jackets and starting their performance proper.

The boy band pose for a photo during a media showcase for their new EP, *Heng:garæ*, at a hotel in southern Seoul in June, 2020

2021
MAINSTREAM DOMINANCE

Chart-topping albums *Your Choice* and *Attacca* solidified Seventeen's place as a top-tier group, with both EPs achieving millions of sales.

The lyrics of *Your Choice* were especially written to cheer up fans stuck at home due to the restrictions brought in because of the worldwide Covid 19 pandemic. As Seungkwan said, 'We thought the message of love could really console people and resonate with them, especially in these tough times that we're having.'

The lead single "Ready to Love" was recognised by *Billboard* as one of the '25 Best K-Pop Songs of 2021', winning praise for its buzzing, electro-pop production.

Your Choice gave the group their third consecutive million-selling EP, which charted in 11 countries.

There would not be a fourth one-million seller – because within four months came the group's ninth mini-album, the *Attacca* EP, which sold two million copies! This made it the group's first double million-selling album.

Released on 22 October 2021, *Attacca*, marked a significant evolution in the group's musical journey, embracing a more mature and passionate sound. The album's title, derived from the Italian musical term meaning 'to attack' or 'to proceed without pause', reflected the seamless flow and intensity of the six-track album.

Attacca has been widely acclaimed for its cohesive exploration of passionate themes and its bold foray into pop-rock territory. NME highlighted the album as 'an exercise in reinvention', noting its departure from Seventeen's earlier bubbly pop tracks and commending the group's growth and maturity.

Teen Vogue emphasised the album's portrayal of love as 'loud, passionate, and unapologetic', praising the group's commitment to evolving their sound while maintaining their identity. The publication also noted the album's seamless blend of genres, resulting in a dynamic and engaging listening experience.

The album debuted at #13 on the US Billboard 200 chart, marking Seventeen's highest ever ranking on the chart to date, and also becoming their first to spend two consecutive weeks on the chart. Its lead single, the catchy pop-rock anthem "Rock With You", which blended rock elements with the group's signature polished sound, quickly rose to the top of multiple Korean real-time music charts, including Bugs, Melon, and Genie. Internationally, the song reached #1 on iTunes Top Songs charts in at least 19 different regions, including Argentina and Peru.

Seventeen perform on stage during the 30th High1 Seoul Music Awards in Seoul, South Korea in January, 2021

2022

GROWING GLOBAL APPEAL

Then in 2022, *Face the Sun* and its repackaged and expanded version *Sector 17*, broke sales records and charted globally, including on the US Billboard 200.

Face the Sun was an especially apt title as it was released in May 2022 when fans were able to leave their houses and pick up their normal lives post-pandemic. Key tracks were the lead single "Hot", a powerful and intense anthem with a Western-inspired hip-hop sound, and "Darl+ing", Seventeen's first full English-language single, a soft pop song with a comforting melody, expressing themes of togetherness and connection.

In all, the album featured nine tracks that explored themes of ambition, struggle, and self-discovery.

A few months later, in July, *Face the Sun* was repackaged as *Sector 17*, with four additional tracks to expand on the original album's themes, while introducing new music and a fresh perspective on Seventeen's journey. The repackage continued the narrative of self-discovery and ambition, but with a shift from the intensity of *Face the Sun* to a brighter, more hopeful outlook.

Key among the additional tracks were "World", an upbeat, summery track, and "Cheers" which was a hip-hop anthem by the Leaders sub-unit of S.Coups, Woozi, and Hoshi, celebrating their hard-earned success.

"World" made the top ten domestically and reached #79 on the US iTunes chart.

While *Face the Sun* had debuted at #7 on the Billboard 200 chart, marking Seventeen's first entry into the chart's Top 10, the repackage did even better and arrived in at #4 on the Billboard 200, setting a new peak for the group.

Tracks from the album were a big feature of 2022's Be The Sun tour which grossed over US$63m and sold 542,000 tickets, according to the allkpop online platform. These concerts marked the group's return to live performances after the Covid-19 pandemic.

The 29-date tour which ran from June to December 2022 spanned 17 cities across Asia and North America including Tokyo and Osaka in Japan, Jakarta in Indonesia, Vancouver and Toronto in Canada, and Los Angeles, Seattle, Houston, Chicago, Atlanta, and Washington DC in the USA. Their stop at Bocaue in the Philippines saw them become the first K-pop act to perform in the Philippine Arena, the largest indoor arena in the world with a capacity of 55,000 seats.

Throughout the tour came widespread acclaim for the group's high-energy performances and meticulous choreography.

Seventeen's 4th album *Face the Sun* press release at the Conrad Seoul Grand Ballroom in May, 2022 in Seoul, South Korea

2023

MAKING HISTORY

Seventeen's 2023 album *FML* became the best-selling K-pop album in history and in the world that year.

Their 10th EP, *FML* had phenomenal pre-orders totalling over 4.6 million copies, setting a record for the most pre-ordered album in South Korean history at the time. It remains to this day, the second most pre-ordered album ever domestically. The album sold 3.9 million copies on its first day, breaking records for first day and first week sales.

By the end of its first week, *FML* had sold over 4.5 million copies worldwide, and it went on to become the first K-pop album to surpass 6 million copies sold. With eventual global sales of 6.4 million units, *FML* was listed as the best-selling album worldwide by the International Federation of the Phonographic Industry (IFPI) renowned for its accreditation system.

The K-POP boy band surrounded by fans as they perform at the UNESCO headquarters in Paris, November 2023

It debuted at #2 on the US Billboard 200 album chart, making it the group's third US Top 10 release.

Exploring themes of emotional vulnerability, self-reflection, and personal growth, the album delved into the complexities of life and relationships, including feelings of frustration, heartache, and resilience. Tracks like "F*ck My Life" address intense emotional struggles, while others, like "Super", focus on empowerment and self-expression. The album's raw, introspective lyrics contrast with an energetic, genre-blending overall sound.

Critics felt that it demonstrated Seventeen's maturity and ability to evolve both musically and thematically and pointed out their refined sound and maturity, with the album's blend of pop, hip-hop, and rock elements being particularly well-received. Fans and critics alike commended the group for taking bold steps in both lyricism and music production. The Associated Press review highlighted the album's authenticity, stating it 'feels remarkably true to them: a celebration of their success, and the motivation to push harder in the future.'

This was followed up in October by the group's 11th EP *Seventeenth Heaven* – a dance-heavy collection of eight tracks, produced by Woozi and Bumzu, which had over 5.2 million pre-orders, making it the most pre-ordered K-pop album in history. Its lead single "God of Music" became the group's first single to top the South Korean Circle Digital Chart, making its debut at #1.

Among several accolades, *Seventeenth Heaven* won the group Artist of the Year (Album) at the 2024 South Korean Circle Chart Music awards.

The group also continued with its Follow tour which visited five cities across Japan and three cities in Asia, starting in July 2023 and ending in May 2024.

2024

THE HITS KEEP COMING

In 2024, the group's third compilation album (the second in their native language) *17 Is Right Here* included every Korean-language single they had ever released. The double CD version also included Korean versions of their Japanese-language singles. *17 is Right Here sold* over 2 million copies on the day of its release, setting a new record for K-pop compilation album sales. It peaked at #5 on the US Billboard 200 albums chart and at #1 on the Billboard World Albums listings – making it the group's 10th number one on that chart.

Although largely a greatest-hits-style release, the album did include four new tracks; "Maestro", a dance R&B number written by a Seventeen team led by Woozi , "Spell" (performed by the performance team) "Cheers to Youth" (performed by the vocal team) and "Lalali" (performed by the hip-hop team).

"Maestro" was the lead single and has gone on to become one of the group's biggest ever hits. It is also one of their most ambitious, mixing sweet vocals and fast-paced rapping with piano riffs and unexpected rhythmical switches. It gave the group its first ever UK Top 40 hit in May 2024 – peaking at #26.

And just months after wrapping up the Follow tour, the group hit the road again on their Right Here world tour, running from October 2024 until February 2025, taking in South Korea, Japan, Asia, plus 10-dates in the United States, including their first stadium show in Los Angeles.

Among the wholly positive reviews, American critics variously described the concerts as 'electrifying' (*Melodic Magazine*); 'flawless choreography and an impressive visual spectacle' (*San Francisco Chronicle*) and 'demonstrating their bond and confidence' (Consequence pop culture site).

The set list included new tracks from the group's 13th EP *Spill the Feels*, including lead track "Love, Money, Fame", featuring Grammy award-winning American music producer DJ Khaled. The EP surpassed three million pre-orders within two weeks of its release being announced. In its review, *NME* said the album showed that Seventeen had 'an unwavering commitment to spreading hope, joy, and love, all via addictive and affecting music'.

However, although they had both worked on the music for *Spill the Feels*, neither Jeonghan or Jun were able to promote the album nor join the tour. Jun was away on an acting job in China, while Jeonghan had to enlist in the military, as is standard for young men in South Korea.

eonghan, Mingyu, Hoshi, and Vernon visit the Empire State Building in New York to celebrate the release of their mini album Spill the Feels in October, 2024

2025

TENTH & TIMELESS

The tenth year has already seen Seventeen at full speed, releasing fresh projects and celebrating a decade of impact. They treated Carats to their sub-unit BSS dropping *Teleparty* in January, where swing-jazz meets party vibes. March also saw a debut from Hoshi x Woozi as *Beam* burst out, featuring intense choreography and a blast of hip-hop in "96ers".

On January 21, 2025, Seventeen unveiled "Bad Influence", a track produced by Pharrell Williams and presented during the Louis Vuitton Fall/Winter 2025 Men's Collection show at Paris Fashion Week. This collaboration marks a significant fusion of K-pop and high fashion.

Interactive events were equally as exciting, from Instagram lives with 50K+ fans cheering them on, to a massive fan-meeting dubbed SEVENTEEN in CARAT LAND at Incheon's stadium, where heartfelt updates flew as Hoshi and Woozi shared their upcoming military plans.

But the real fireworks ignited on May 26 – their 10th anniversary exploded into existence with *Happy Burstday*, a full-group album with 16 tracks (solo tracks included) and the title track "Thunder," scoring multiple trophies and going straight to #1 on Korea's charts.

They celebrated with a bridge-top concert at Jamsu Bridge, global listening parties, and even an Airbnb takeover for 60 lucky Carats – plus now a two-part special on *Going Seventeen.*

Marking their 10th year, Seventeen have wasted no time in 2025 with new music releases, standout moments, and major milestones – and there's no telling what else they've got up their sleeves.

Seventeen attend the 39th Golden Disc Awards at Mizuho PayPay Dome in Fukuoka, where they won Album of the Year (Disc Daesang), on January 5, 2025

STANDING OUT AS SELF-PRODUCING IDOLS

Seventeen live on stage at the 2024 Billboard Music Awards

THE GROUP'S IDENTITY as self-producing idols sets them apart from other K-pop groups. This term refers to the group's active involvement in all aspects of their music and performances, including songwriting, composing, producing, and choreographing. While many K-pop artists rely heavily on external producers, choreographers, and creative directors, Seventeen's hands-on approach is relatively rare in the industry and has allowed them an autonomy which has shaped their identity and music.

Key members, including producer Woozi, group leader S.Coups, and choreographer Hoshi, each play a pivotal role in songwriting, choreography, and production, taking centre stage in shaping the group's identity and crafting Seventeen's music and performances.

Many K-pop groups are crafted and managed by entertainment companies that oversee every detail, from music production to choreography and styling. While this system ensures consistency and professionalism, it often limits direct input from the idols themselves. While Seventeen work closely with their agency, Pledis Entertainment, to ensure their creative vision aligns with their output, their agreement allows each group member to explore their strengths and contribute to different facets of their artistry and gives them a greater sense of ownership and authenticity.

As Wonwoo told *Billboard* in a 2019 interview; 'Since the very beginning, every time before we release our music, we come together for a meeting and discuss what story we want to tell, what narrative fits us right now, and what the public wants to hear. We then personalise these ideas. It's always been like that.'

The group's three unit structure further reinforces their self-producing identity, as each sub-unit has specific creative responsibilities.

As leader of the vocal team, Woozi is Seventeen's primary composer and producer. He has been involved in creating most of their discography, amounting to some 140 tracks, and shaping their musical identity. His work ensures that the group maintains a cohesive and authentic sound.

Other members like S.Coups, Hoshi, and Vernon also contribute to lyrics and concepts, infusing their music with personal stories and unique perspectives.

Hoshi, the leader of the performance team, is known for creating much of Seventeen's choreography. The group's signature synchronised performances and intricate formations are a result of his vision and the collaborative input of the Performance team, and other members often contribute to the conceptualisation of their music videos, stage performances, and album designs.

Choreography such as that used for "Don't Wanna Cry "and "Home;Run" exemplify their creativity and focus on storytelling through dance.

Seventeen's self-producing model allows them to stay true to their artistic vision while also adapting to evolving trends. This creative freedom is rare in the highly structured K-pop world and has earned them widespread respect within the industry. Critics and fans alike praise their authenticity, work ethic, and ability to continuously innovate.

Their self-producing approach is often cited as a factor in their ability to maintain a distinct identity over a decade.

Seventeen perform in concert during their Ode to You tour at the Prudential Center in Newark, New Jersey, in January 2020

THE BENEFITS OF SELF-PRODUCING

THE BENEFITS OF SELF-PRODUCING

ARTISTIC IDENTITY:

Seventeen's music and performances feel personal and unique, reflecting the members' personalities and experiences.

FAN CONNECTION:

Carats appreciate the group's dedication to creating music and performances for them. This effort strengthens the bond between the group and their fans.

INDUSTRY INFLUENCE:

Seventeen has set a precedent for what K-pop idols can achieve when given creative freedom. Their success has inspired other groups and agencies to explore more collaborative approaches.

Two creatives who work closely with Seventeen are music producers Bumzu and Park Kitae.

Bumzu is a prominent South Korean singer, songwriter, and record producer whose innovative approach to music production has played a big part in Seventeen's success.

BUMZU

Born on 8 November 1991 in Seoul, his musical journey began in Seoul's underground music scene during his high school years, where he honed his skills and developed a passion for music production. Bumzu's mainstream breakthrough came in 2011 when he composed "Don't Go, Go Away" for Jang Woo-hyuk.

Following his appearance in the South Korean singing competition *Superstar K 4*, when he was just 22 years old, Bumzu came to the attention of Pledis Entertainment and began collaborating with several of their artists, including Seventeen. He has played a pivotal role in shaping the group's musical direction since their debut. Working closely with Woozi, Bumzu co-produced their debut track *Adore U* and has continued to contribute significantly to their discography.

Bumzu's contributions to Seventeen's music are characterised by a blend of K-pop and R&B influences, crafting a distinctive sound that appeals to a global audience. His production credits include some of the group's biggest hits including *Fear*, *Home;Run*, and *Left & Right*.

In recognition of his prolific work, Bumzu was awarded the Grand Prize by the Korea Music Copyright Association (KOMCA) in 2024, acknowledging him as the highest-earning songwriter for K-pop in 2023.

Beyond his work with Seventeen, Bumzu co-founded the music production company Prismfilter Music Group in 2020, further solidifying his influence in the industry.

Seventeen perform during a showcase for their fifth mini album *You Make My Day* in Seoul on July 16, 2018

The group's other key producer is Park Kitae, also known professionally as 'Prism Filter'. He is a distinguished South Korean music video director and visual artist renowned for his innovative work in the K-pop industry. As the founder of the creative agency Prism Filter, Park has been instrumental in crafting visually compelling narratives that complement the musical artistry of various K-pop acts, most notably Seventeen.

Park's collaboration with Seventeen has been pivotal in defining the group's visual identity. He has directed several of their music videos, each characterised by meticulous attention to detail, dynamic cinematography, and a deep understanding of the group's concept and choreography. His work on music videos such as "Home;Run", "Left & Right", and "Ready to Love" has been particularly acclaimed, seamlessly blending storytelling with performance to enhance the group's musical expression.

ABOVE & OPP PAGE: Stills taken from Seventeen's "Left & Right" official music video directed by Park Kitae

In addition to music videos, Park Kitae has directed various other visual content for Seventeen, including promotional materials, concert VCRs, and behind-the-scenes documentaries. His holistic approach ensures a consistent and engaging visual experience for fans, reinforcing the group's brand identity across multiple platforms.

Park's creative vision extends beyond traditional music video production. He often incorporates innovative techniques and experimental aesthetics, pushing the boundaries of visual storytelling in K-pop. His ability to adapt to different musical genres and group concepts has made him a sought-after director in the industry.

Park has significantly contributed to Seventeen's global appeal, creating visuals that resonate with a wide audience. His work not only amplifies the group's musical talents but also adds a rich, visual dimension that enhances the overall fan experience.

His innovative direction and artistic sensibilities have been instrumental in shaping the group's visual narrative, contributing to their success and influence in the global music scene.

NOTHING INSIDE
NOTHING INSIDE
NOTHING INSIDE
NOTHING INSIDE
NOTHING INSIDE

SEVENTEEN'S SUB-UNITS

SEVENTEEN'S SUB-UNITS

BEYOND THEIR PRIMARY STRUCTURE of vocal, rap, and performance units, Seventeen members have explored diverse creative outlets through sub-unit projects. These sub-units allow members to showcase different facets of their artistry and connect with fans in fresh, exciting ways.

Regardless of the genre, if the main group members agree that a track is more suitable for a sub-unit rather than the full group, the track is further developed to better suit the sub-unit's character.

Sub-unit tracks are regularly included in Seventeen's albums and EPs, so listening to them is an easy way to discover more about each unit and its individual members. As group leader S. Coups told *Billboard* in 2019; 'When we're performing in units, it shows a different colour from when we perform as a group. Each member has their own charm and ability, and through these units we're able to show different sides to ourselves'.

'Through our units we're able to show off different styles of music that we weren't able to show as a group as a whole, so that's why I think units are really, really important to our group,' added Joshua.

S.Coups of Seventeen during a showcase for their mini album *Heng:garæ* at Intercontinental Coex in Seoul, South Korea in June 2020

BSS

The trio BSS (short for BooSeokSoon) comprising members Hoshi, DK and Seungkwan, first joined up as a sub team in 2018 with the high-energy single "Just Do It". Since then they have proved a big hit with fans. These three group members are among the most extroverted of Seventeen and like to add a playful and comedic twist to their performance style.

But fans had to wait five years for a follow-up track as BSS didn't deliver their second offering, the *Second Wind* EP, until 2023. These songs aimed to energise listeners during various times of the day, beginning with the title track, the powerful wake-up call "Fighting", going through to a midday vibe with "Lunch" and finishing with the laid back lullaby of "7pm". *Second Wind* sold 478,000 copies on day one of its release on 6 February, breaking the record for a release by a K-pop sub-unit. BSS also achieved their first music show win with "Fighting" on *Show Champion*.

The sub-unit's second single album *Teleparty* and lead track *CBZ* (*Prime Time*) were released on 8 January 2025.

DK has spoken of wanting to lead the K-pop industry as a 'fourth generation' group. Each of the member's roles in BSS are different from their roles in the main Seventeen group, so that each of the trio has the chance to show off various aspects of their personality and talent in the different groups. For example Seungkwan is the maknae (youngest member) in BSS, whereas that role goes to Dino in Seventeen. DK is the leader of BSS, whereas Hoshi is more senior in Seventeen.

HOSHI
DK
SEUNGKWAN

S. COUPS

SVT LEADERS

This sub-unit features S.Coups, Woozi, and Hoshi, representing the leaders of Seventeen's three main units. Together, they have an incredible collaborative synergy. Tracks like "Change Up" showcase their ability to blend styles, while reinforcing the group's unified vision.

JEONGHAN X WONWOO (JxW)

A newer pairing within the Seventeen universe, JxW- Jeonghan and Wonwoo's collaboration - highlights a more introspective and melodic style. Their album *This Man* came out on 17 June 2024, and within a week had broken the record set by their fellow Seventeen idols in BSS for first week sales by a K-pop sub-unit by achieving 787,046 sales. The album also peaked at #3 on South Korea's Circle album chart.

JEONGHAN

WONWOO
Changes

FML

SEVENTEEN'S *FML* ALBUM, released in April 2023, marked a significant milestone in the group's career and the K-pop industry as a whole. The album broke numerous records, set new industry benchmarks, and garnered widespread acclaim for its innovative musicality and emotional resonance. It was simply a remarkable body of work.

Released in April 2023, *FML* became the best-selling album in K-pop history and the biggest selling record of the year, exceeding six million copies sold within its first week of release. It reached quadruple million-seller status on its debut day, a record-breaking achievement.

The EP, the group's 10th, also set a new record for the most pre-ordered album in South Korean history, at 4.64 million copies. It entered the US Billboard 200 chart at #2 with 135,000 album-equivalent units becoming Seventeen's third Top 10 release and its highest charting album in the US overall. It went on to top major global music charts and dominated iTunes charts in over 30 countries. It also won album of the year at the MAMAs (Asian music artist awards).

The album as a whole explores the theme of self-discovery, resilience, and empowerment, reflecting the group's artistic growth and maturity almost 10 years on from their debut. The tracks feature a dynamic blend of genres, including hip-hop, pop, and R&B, showcasing Seventeen's signature style and evolution and balancing bold experimentation with mass appeal.

Its two lead singles, "FML" and "Super" were completely opposite to each other, the hard-hitting "FML" being unusually downbeat, while rock anthem "Super" was more typically upbeat and celebratory in its style. Both tracks went viral with hashtags like #SEVENTEEN_FML and #SEVENTEEN_SUPER trending globally.

Dance challenges based on the album's choreography became wildly popular on TikTok and Instagram.

Praised for its lyrical depth and cohesive production, *FML* was highlighted by major outlets such as *Rolling Stone* and *NME* for its artistic maturity. *The Korea Herald* described *FML* as 'a cultural moment', cementing Seventeen's legacy in K-pop.

FML track listing

F*ck My Life

Super

Fire

I Don't Understand But I Luv U

Dust

April shower

Overall the album's versatility and bold approach earned it widespread recognition, with critics lauding Seventeen's ability to balance commercial appeal with artistic integrity.

The tracks from *FML* became the centrepiece of Seventeen's Follow tour, where live renditions were met with rave reviews. Fans loved the way the group brought the album's emotional depth to life on stage through enthusiastic performances, explosive energy, and intricate choreography. The innovative choreography and lyrical depth further proved Seventeen's reputation as a powerhouse in performance and storytelling.

The album also resonated deeply with Carats, for its authentic storytelling and relatable lyrics - fans appreciating the group's commitment to exploring mental health and perseverance, creating a sense of shared understanding, and helping to normalise discussions about mental health struggles.

In an interview with the UK's BBC before Seventeen's historic Glastonbury festival appearance, Wonwoo, speaking through a translator, said 'When we were putting together the album, some of the members were going through a rough time. Our mindset is reflected in the songs. When we honestly, openly, talk about our feelings it really helps to get rid of the negativity.'

Seventeen bring the stage to life during the 12th Circle Chart Music Awards at the KSPO Dome on February 18, 2023 in Seoul, South Korea

WINNING OVER THE WORLD

WINNING OVER THE WORLD

Fans in the crowd ready for Seventeen's performance on the Pyramid Stage at Glastonbury Festival in England on June 28, 2024

사랑해요
HI MUM
사랑해요
MOLLY ♥ SEVENTEEN
사랑해요
사랑해요
R THE WORLD

AS SEVENTEEN'S POPULARITY has soared, so has their reach. Seventeen's global tours, sold-out concerts, and international fan events are spectacles now making waves far beyond South Korea.

Through their music and performances, they've bridged cultural divides, proving that their artistry transcends language and borders.

Celebrated for their synchronised choreography and electrifying stage presence, Seventeen's live performances are masterclasses in precision and charisma, as well as playing a key role in boosting album sales. Their sweet interactions with audiences are becoming legendary and other popular features of their concerts are onstage dance breaks and battles - even riff offs.

The idols in Seventeen are consummate live performers who insist on making sure their audiences leave their shows with the feeling that they need to see the group again and again.

No two shows are the same, as Seventeen entertain - even adding comedy and skits to their three-hour set.

Seventeen performing during the 12th Circle Chart Music Awards at the KSPO Dome on February 18, 2023 in Seoul, South Korea

Right Here – Set list

The following is from their performance on 13 October 2024, at the 41,000 seater Goyang Stadium in South Korea:

1. Fear
2. Fearless
3. Maestro
4. Ash
5. Crush
6. Water (Hip-Hop Unit)
7. Monster (Hip-Hop Unit)
8. Rain (Performance Unit)
9. Lilili Yabbay (Performance Unit)
10. Candy (Vocal Unit)
11. Cheers to Youth (Vocal Unit)
12. Our Dawn is Hotter than Day
13. Not Alone (Korean version)
14. Oh My!
15. Snap Shoot
16. God of Music
17. Ima (Even If the World Ends Tomorrow) [Korean version]
18. Home
19. Love, Money, Fame
20. March
21. Super
22. Encore:

Adore U
'Bout You
Campfire
If You Leave Me
Very Nice

Setlists can vary between performances and locations. For instance, during the US leg of the tour, songs like "Not Alone", "Our Dawn is Hotter than Day", and "Ima (Even If the World Ends Tomorrow)" were omitted. Additionally, encores often featured different combinations of tracks such as "Very Nice", "Hit", "Call Call Call!", "Snap Shoot", "Hot", "Fighting", "Holiday", "Back It Up", "Cheers", "Eyes on You", and "Healing". These variations show Seventeen's adaptability and their efforts to tailor performances to different audiences across the globe.

TOURS AND KEY LIVE PERFORMANCES

SHINING DIAMONDS WORLD TOUR 30 July 2016 – 11 September 2016.
(17 shows in Asia and Oceania in support of albums *17 Carat*, *Boys Be* and *Love & Letter*.)

DIAMOND EDGE WORLD TOUR 14 July 2017- 6 October 2017.
(17 shows in Asia, North America, and South America in support of *Al1* and *Teen, Age*.)

SVT JAPAN TOUR 21 February 2018 – 8 March 2018.
(6 shows in Asia in support of *Al1*, *Teen, Age* and *You Make My Day*.)

IDEAL CUT TOUR 28 June 2018 – 4 November.
(18 shows in Asia in support of *Al1*, *Teen, Age* and *You Make My Day*.)

HARU JAPAN TOUR 2 April 2019 – 27 April 2019.
(12 shows in Asia in support of *We Make You*, *You Make My Day* and *You Made My Dawn*.)

ODE TO YOU WORLD TOUR 30 August 2019 – 8 February 2020.
(24 shows in Asia and North America in support of *An Ode*.)

BE THE SUN WORLD TOUR 25 June 2022 – 28 December 2022.
(29 shows in Asia and North America in support of *Face the Sun* and *Sector 17*.)

FOLLOW WORLD TOUR 21 July 2023 – 26 May 2024.
(28 shows in Asia in support of *FML*, *Always Yours*, *Seventeenth Heaven* and *17 Is Right Here*.)

RIGHT HERE WORLD TOUR 12 October 2024 – 16 February 2025.
(30 shows in Asia and North America in support of *Spill the Feels*.)

Seventeen performs in concert during their Ode to You tour at the Prudential Center on January 10, 2020 in Newark, New Jersey

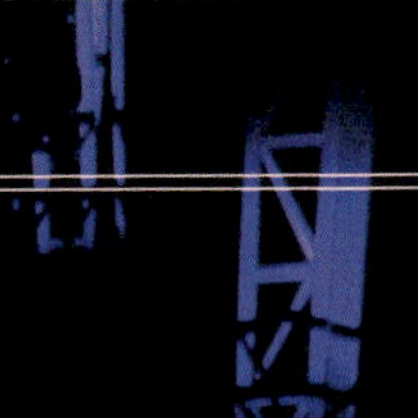

Ode to You

OTHER KEY APPEARANCES....

GLASTONBURY, UK
JUNE 2024

Seventeen's appearance at Glastonbury on 23 June 2024 was nothing short of a triumph. Not only did they make history as the first K-pop group to play the main Pyramid stage, but they completely won over the crowd which largely comprised people who knew little about them – or K-pop more generally – when their hour-long set began.

Save a few diehard Carats, most Glastonbury goers were new to the precision choreography and catchy chants of Seventeen's performance. Although they are more used to long concerts – often lasting up to three hours – the group excelled at curating a compact selection of their biggest and most accessible hits for the Pyramid stage, including "Maestro", "Lalali", "Hot", and "2 Minus 1" – all performed with the energy and enthusiasm their established fanbase has come to expect.

By the end of the set they had a crowd of new fans jumping around and joining in with the famous repeated final chorus of "Very Nice". The continuation of the song with another burst of the refrain after it has apparently finished has become something of an in-joke with fans and translated perfectly to the UK festival audience.

'Recently, most of our performances have taken place in indoor venues, so playing the wide-open outdoor stage at Glastonbury was a rare and exciting experience,' rapper Wonwoo told *NME*. 'It was a great opportunity to showcase our music and energy in a new setting for a fresh crowd.

'Even though the language, country and culture are all different, we can still connect as one, through music. We are just extremely honoured to be here'.

The BBC's review of the group's performance said that, 'Seungkwan and Hoshi were the most exuberant, riling up the crowd during and between songs, while Woozi's airy vocals were juxtaposed with Vernon and Joshua's more soulful tones. But it was the songs with guitar riffs and easily-chanted English lyrics that fared best - among them, the rap-heavy track "Lalali" and the rock "2 Minus 1".'

Seventeen perform on Glastonbury's Pyramid Stage in Somerset, England, on June 28, 2024

ROCK WITH YOU

Glasto set list

Maestro

Ready To Love

SOS

Rock With You

2 Minus 1
(Joshua & Vernon)

I Don't Understand But I Luv U
(Performance Unit)

Cheers To Youth

Lalali

Clap

Hot

Headliner

God Of Music

Very Nice

Seventeen perform on Glastonbury's Pyramid Stage in Somerset, England, on June 28, 2024

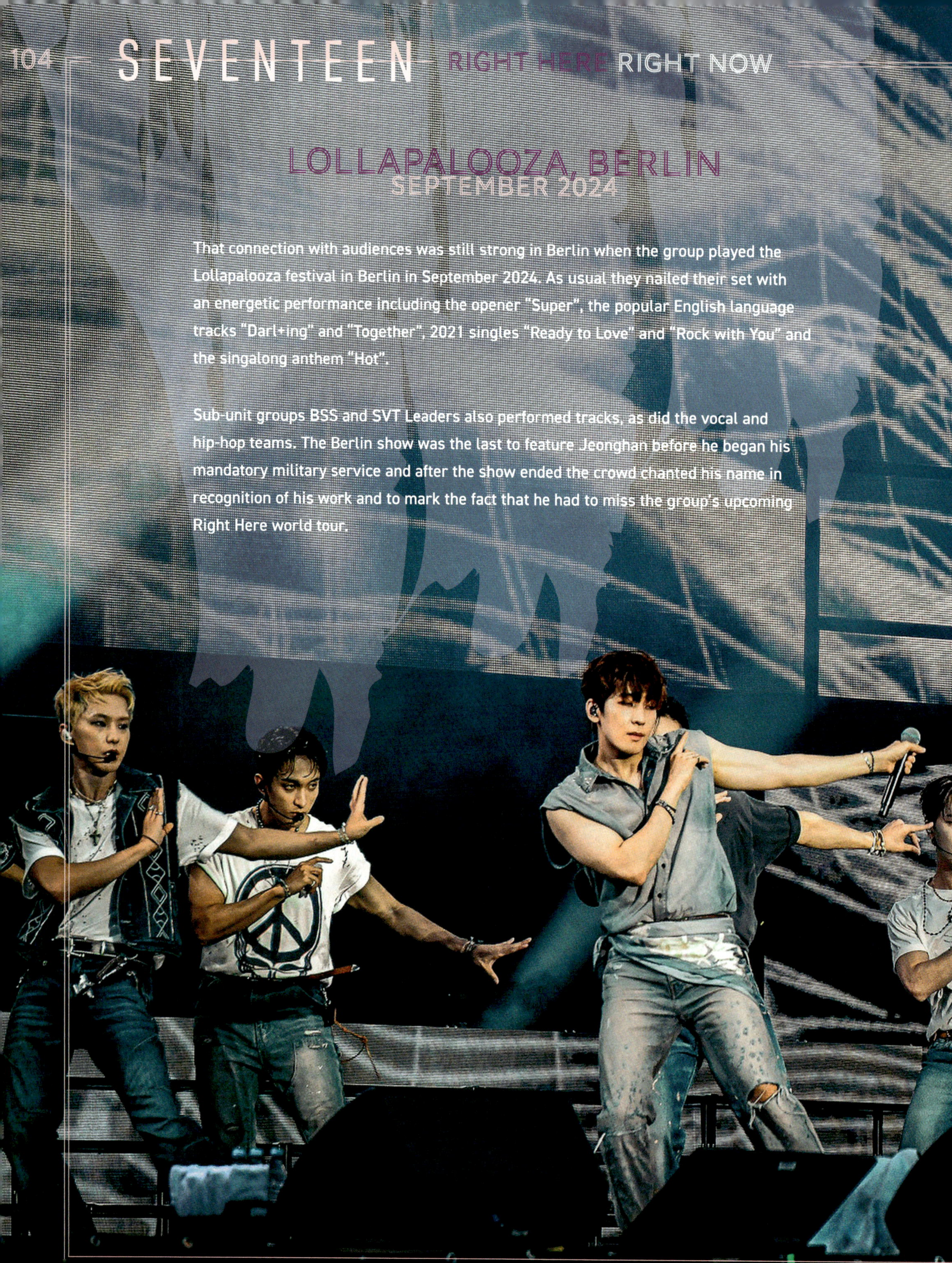

LOLLAPALOOZA, BERLIN
SEPTEMBER 2024

That connection with audiences was still strong in Berlin when the group played the Lollapalooza festival in Berlin in September 2024. As usual they nailed their set with an energetic performance including the opener "Super", the popular English language tracks "Darl+ing" and "Together", 2021 singles "Ready to Love" and "Rock with You" and the singalong anthem "Hot".

Sub-unit groups BSS and SVT Leaders also performed tracks, as did the vocal and hip-hop teams. The Berlin show was the last to feature Jeonghan before he began his mandatory military service and after the show ended the crowd chanted his name in recognition of his work and to mark the fact that he had to miss the group's upcoming Right Here world tour.

WHAT THE CRITICS SAY

WHAT THE CRITICS SAY

The reviews for Seventeen's concerts just get better and better. Here are some for their Right Here world tour, for which the group was down to 11 members, with Jeonghan away enlisting for his mandatory military service, and Jun on hiatus to focus on acting back in China.

'A sonic masterpiece, showcasing Seventeen's impeccable musicianship and undeniable stage presence.' *Korea Joongang Daily* on the group's opening show in Goyang, South Korea.

'Electrifying'. *Melodic Magazine*, on the New York UBS Arena shows.

'Flawless choreography ... an impressive visual spectacle'. *San Francisco Chronicle*.

Seventeen on stage at the Lollapalooza Festival in Berlin, 2024

STADIUM DEBUT IN LOS ANGELES
NOVEMBER 2024

Seventeen performed two sold-out shows at the BMO Stadium in Los Angeles in November 2024 to wrap up their American tour. LA is Joshua's hometown and while he was there he received a certificate awarded to the group by the local city council with thanks for running the 'Seventeen the City Los Angeles' project. This project saw downtown LA decorated with Seventeen-themed displays in the group's colours of rose quartz and serenity (sky blue).

Seventeen members The8, Woozi, Dino, Wonwoo, Joshua, Vernon, DK, Hoshi, Mingyu, Seungkwan, and S.Coups perform live onstage at BMO Stadium in Los Angeles, California, on November 9, 2024

K-POP UNPACKED

K-POP UNPACKED

K-POP'S DOMINANCE in the global music industry is no longer up for debate, but for many Western audiences, the mechanics of its success remain a mystery.

At the heart of South Korea's music industry lies a unique, fast-paced and highly competitive system of weekly televised music shows, which serve as both promotional platforms and performance arenas for K-pop artists. These programmes, where artists perform and compete for highly coveted 'wins', have been a staple of the industry since the 1990s, shaping careers and solidifying fan engagement.

It's a concept with no true equivalent in the West and so understanding it requires more than just watching performances; it means diving into the world of 'comebacks', 'encore stages', 'triple crowns', and other K-pop-specific jargon. Unpacking the history, impact, and insider terminology of South Korea's music show phenomenon, reveals why a single win on a show can make all the difference for an artist's career. These music shows play a vital role in a group's success and visibility, as a 'win' often serves as a benchmark of an act's popularity and influence. More than just a promotional tool, these music shows are key battlegrounds where artists and idols fight to push their music up the charts. This South Korean system rewards artists weekly based on a mix of digital performance, album sales, social media engagement, and real-time voting, quite unlike the Western music industry, where awards are often given at annual ceremonies.

While Korean fans have long understood the weight of these music show wins, international audiences are still catching up, discovering just how influential these shows are — not just as entertainment, but as a key driver of K-pop's commercial and cultural power. While Western artists typically rely on album launches, social media engagement, and press appearances to promote their work, in South Korea, securing music show wins is a formalised and expected part of a promotional campaign.

South Korea has several major music shows, each hosted by different television networks and including: *The Show* (SBS MTV, Tuesdays) *Show Champion* (MBC M, Wednesdays) *M Countdown* (Mnet, Thursdays) *Music Bank* (KBS, Fridays) *Show! Music Core* (MBC, Saturdays) and *Inkigayo* (SBS, Sundays).

Each of these programmes follow a similar format where the artists perform live (although often pre-recorded for quality control), and at the end of the show, a winner is announced based on a scoring system. While criteria vary slightly by show, the rankings typically consider album sales, digital streaming numbers, broadcast points, social media presence, and fan voting. Winning a music show is not just an honour but a strategic milestone that can significantly boost an artist's reputation, album sales, and public recognition.

Seventeen's rise to the top of the K-pop industry has certainly been fuelled in part by their consistent success on South Korea's music shows, where they have accumulated a remarkable number of wins since their debut in 2015. Their first-ever music show success came in 2016 on *Show Champion* with "Pretty U" – a defining moment in their career. Since then, with each 'comeback', Seventeen has dominated the competition, securing multiple 'triple crowns' and accumulating dozens of trophies across leading shows. These wins are more than just symbolic — they reflect the group's massive album sales, strong digital presence, and fan support. Music shows have also allowed Seventeen to showcase their self-production skills, synchronised choreography, and engaging stage presence, drawing in new fans and reinforcing their credibility in the industry.

Their 2022 release, "Hot", from their *Face the Sun* album, was another major success, earning them multiple music show trophies, including wins on *M Countdown*, *Music Bank*, and *Inkigayo*. This marked their ability to not only perform well digitally but also drive substantial physical album sales, a key factor in scoring. Similarly, their 2023 comeback with *Super* saw them sweep the music shows, reinforcing their dominance in the industry.

While a music show trophy itself may not generate revenue, winning a show significantly impacts an artist's commercial success, generally leading to increased album sales, higher streaming numbers, and greater media exposure. It also enhances an artist's leverage when negotiating endorsements, concert deals, and brand partnerships.

For groups like Seventeen, consistent wins solidify their place in K-pop's upper echelon, maintaining momentum, keeping fans engaged, and proving commercial viability.

The group's strong presence in music shows contributes to their global brand, enabling them to expand beyond South Korea and into international markets.

While traditional TV ratings are modest, international streaming has made music shows far more impactful. *M Countdown*, Music Bank, and *Inkigayo* stream globally via platforms like KOCOWA, Viki, and official YouTube channels, significantly expanding their audience.

K-pop fans worldwide can also watch performances on Weverse, Naver, and TikTok, often driving millions of views per performance. Popular performances from top-tier groups like Seventeen can rack up 10+ million views on YouTube within days.

As well as the views, music shows are crucial for building buzz around a comeback, generating viral moments through trending performances and boosting album and digital sales through visibility.

For groups like Seventeen, just one, well-received performance can drive album sales, increase social media engagement, and reinforce their brand on a global scale. So while these shows may not dominate traditional TV ratings, their influence – especially online – is undeniable.

In short, South Korea's music show system is a high-stakes arena where competition is fierce, and victory is highly valued. For fans and artists alike, each win is not just a trophy - it is a statement of influence, dedication, and success.

Seventeen perform during a showcase for their sixth mini album, *You Made My Dawn*, in Seoul in 2019

Seventeen perform on Glastonbury's Pyramid Stage in Somerset, England, 2024

Seventeen perform at BMO Stadium in Los Angeles on November 9, 2024

DO YOU KNOW YOUR MAKNAE FROM YOUR BIAS WRECKERS?

**The K-pop fandom has many slang terms.
Here's a run down of some of the key words and phrases to know.**

ALL-KILL AND PERFECT ALL-KILL

All-Kill (AK) means a song ranks #1 on all major, real time Korean music charts simultaneously, including Melon, Genie, Bugs, and FLO.

A Perfect All-Kill (PAK) requires a song not only to rank #1 on all charts, but also to maintain the position for an extended period, on both real-time and daily and including iChart's weekly ranking.

Achieving a PAK is a rare accomplishment, signifying that a song is dominating the Korean music market across all platforms.

Seventeen's song "Super", released on 24 April 2023, achieved a #1 All-Kill. Additionally, the sub-unit BSS, comprising Seventeen members Seungkwan, DK, and Hoshi, achieved a #1 All-Kill with their track "Fighting", released on 6 February 2023.

BIAS

A fan's favourite member of a group – the one they'll collect the most merch on.

BIAS WRECKER

The member who could tempt you away!

COMEBACK

Unlike in the West when a comeback would signify the return of a favourite artist after retirement or many years away, in K-pop it's called a comeback whenever an idol group releases new music – be that a single, EP, or full album – or delivers a new concept – anything from a new image to some different choreography.

And the frequency of music releases is also different. Whereas most Western recording artists put out an album sporadically and sometimes not for a few years, the K-pop groups release albums every six to eight months, following a structured promotional cycle. EPs – which are mini albums of half a dozen tracks or less, are also much more common in K-pop than in the Western charts.

So 'comebacks' occur every few months and, despite the frequency, each one is a major event and will usually include a performance on a music show.

For example, Seventeen's comeback with "Super" in 2023 featured a fresh martial-arts-inspired concept and intense choreography, making it one of their most memorable promotions.

DEBUT

The official launch of a group and its members.

ENCORE STAGE

The encore stage occurs after an artist wins a music show. The winning group or soloist performs their song again – often in a more relaxed and playful manner – as a celebration of their victory.

Fans pay close attention to encore stages because they reveal whether idols can sing live without backing tracks. Some groups use this moment to joke around, interact with fans, or deliver impromptu a cappella versions of their songs.

ERA

Another word for a K-pop comeback.

Seventeen light up the stage during their Ode to You tour at Prudential Center in Newark, New Jersey, 2020

FANCAM

A fancam is a video focusing on a single member during a performance, filmed either by fans or official music show staff. Viral fancams can elevate an idol's popularity, especially among international audiences.

Seventeen's Hoshi's fancam for "Super" gained millions of views thanks to his sharp dance moves.

GRAND SLAM

Achieving the 'slam' means winning trophies on the five leading music shows (*Music Bank*, *Inkigayo*, *M Countdown*, *Show! Music Core*, and *Show Champion*) in a single promotion period. Seventeen first achieved this with the single "Home" from their 2019 EP *You Made My Dawn*. In total "Home" won 10 trophies across the shows, including two triple crowns, as well as the 'slam'.

IDOL

K-pop group members are known as 'idols'.

KILLING PART

The 'killing' part is the most iconic section of a song or choreography, often the section fans anticipate the most. Groups frequently rearrange these moments in encore stages for fun.

The 'palm spin' in "Super" has become one of Seventeen's most recognisable killing parts.

MAKNAE

The youngest idol in a group – that's Dino in Seventeen.

MERCH

All the paraphernalia, from photocards to light sticks in the colours and configurations of a group and its biases.

Mingyu of Seventeen attends Bvlgari's exhibition "Eternally Reborn: a journey through art, jewelry and Rome" at Museum Hanmi in Jongno-gu in Seoul, South Korea, 2024

PHOTOCARDS

Also called pocas or PCs, photocards are the paper photos included in physical K-pop albums. In great demand from fans, the 'cards' are most commonly 3 x 2 inch glossy paper photos which can come to be worth many hundreds of dollars.

STAN

An especially enthusiastic fan.

SUB-UNIT

A few members of a group working together to create their own music, like BSS within Seventeen, is a sub-unit. Sometimes the term is used for the members in a group who share a role or responsibilities for a specific skill, such as the members of a vocal or performance team.

TRAINEE

A K-pop star in training, awaiting their debut.

TRIPLE CROWN

A triple crown occurs when a song wins first place three times on the same music show. Many shows, such as *Inkigayo*, retire a song from competition after it achieves a triple crown, meaning it can no longer win. This prevents a single song from dominating the charts indefinitely and gives room for other artists to come through.

Seventeen's "Don't Wanna Cry" secured multiple triple crowns in 2017, proving its widespread popularity.

VISUAL

The name for the idol or idols in a group who best fit the strict Korean standards of beauty, including small facial features and general 'cuteness'. This leads to big fan debates. The 'visuals' of Seventeen are ...many of them! Vernon got lots of attention in the group's earliest days, while Mingyu gets most votes these days – both are official 'faces' of the group - with Jeonghan is also considered a strong visual in Seventeen.

FAN CULTURE AND CARATS

FAN CULTURE AND CARATS

THE RELATIONSHIP BETWEEN SEVENTEEN and their fanbase, known as Carats, is a cornerstone of the group's remarkable success. Beyond making up enthusiastic audiences, Carats play an integral role in Seventeen's journey, embodying a culture of support and collaboration that has become a defining feature of the group's identity and emotional resonance.

Carats are not just fans; they are active participants in Seventeen's narrative and it's this mutual appreciation and innovative engagement which has elevated Seventeen's career.

This passionate community is characterised by dedication, creativity, and sense of unity. From organising fan projects to amplifying Seventeen's music and messages on social media, Carats have established themselves as a vital force in the group's global recognition.

At the simplest level, Carats are renowned for their visually stunning 'Carat Bong' light stick displays at concerts. These synchronised moments, often coordinated by fans, create a shared sense of awe and unity within arenas. At the other end of the scale, Carats have led initiatives in partnership with the group to support various charitable causes, from disaster relief efforts to educational programmes.

Seventeen's dedication to their fans is evident in their multifaceted engagement strategies. The group consistently prioritises accessibility and connection, leveraging digital platforms and live events to foster a sense of intimacy despite their global reach.

As *Billboard* put it in their review of the group's US 2024 stadium debut in Los Angeles, 'It's not a Seventeen show if the spotlight isn't turned on the fans themselves, whether with interactive chants and gestures or big-screen concert sign debuts. But this time, the group dialled that energy up to 100. Even after stepping up from arenas to stadiums, they pointed out specific fans in the stands (wearing tiger onesies and carrot costumes, among other getups) to dance-battle the members over a song of their choice.'

Over the years, the group has cultivated countless memorable moments with Carats. Seventeen's active presence on digital platforms like Weverse, Twitter, and Instagram allows them to interact directly with fans. From behind-the-scenes updates to heartfelt messages, the group ensures Carats feel seen and valued.

Then the group frequently host fan meetings and high-touch events, offering opportunities for personal interaction. These gatherings often feature games, Q&A sessions, and special performances, reinforcing the group's appreciation for their supporters.

The idols also share glimpses of their personalities and daily lives through vlogs, livestreams, and reality show appearances, and this transparency deepens the emotional connection between the group and its fans.

The Impact of such amazing fan support is not to be underestimated and has significantly shaped Seventeen's trajectory. The enthusiastic streaming, voting, and promotional efforts of Carats have propelled the group's collection of numerous accolades and chart-topping achievements. On top of this, Carats' feedback often informs Seventeen's creative decisions, demonstrating the reciprocal nature of their relationship.

For instance, the overwhelming response to introspective tracks like "Thanks" and "F*ck My Life" has underscored the emotional resonance between Seventeen and their audience. This feedback loop of mutual inspiration ensures the group's artistry remains both authentic and impactful.

In fact the bond between Seventeen and Carats is a model of modern fan/artist relationships. Rooted in mutual respect and shared values, this dynamic has fostered a thriving community that amplifies the group's success while enriching the fan experience. It's a testament to the power of unity and connection in the music industry.

Fans queue up to buy the new album *17 is Right Here* outside a convenience store in the trendy Hongdae neighbourhood of Seoul on April 29, 2024, the day of the album's official release

Seventeen make history by attending their nomination ceremony as Goodwill Ambassadors for Youth at UNESCO headquarters on June 26, 2024 in Paris, France

GOOD WORKS

Beneficiaries of Seventeen and Carats' works include the Social Welfare 'Letters from Angels' campaign in South Korea, Childfund Korea, Plastic Bank, humanitarian NGO Good Neighbors and Korea's Global Education Sharing Project.

Collectively and individually the group and its members have donated, designed, and signed clothing and artworks for charity events.

Group members have also given speeches and performances at events including the UNESCO YOUTH FORUM at the UNESCO HQ in France to encourage awareness and fundraising in November 2023. They were the first K-pop group to run a dedicated session and took the opportunity to explain their #educationcanchange fund-raising initiative which, with the support of the Carat fandom and with a donation from the group's tour profits, has built a school in Malawi. In the future the group has plans to build more schools in the world's least developed countries.

JOSHUA

INSPIRING AND VISIONARY

INSPIRING AND VISIONARY

SEVENTEEN'S IMPACT WITHIN THE ever-evolving K-pop landscape stands out for inspiring a wave of artist-led approaches in the genre.

The group's emphasis on self-production is solidifying their place as pioneers as the group's leaders - S.Coups, Woozi, and Hoshi - guide their units with remarkable vision.

Woozi's role as the group's main producer has particularly underscored the group's commitment to authenticity, with tracks that deeply resonate with their global audience. This approach is influencing other idols and trainees to take active roles in shaping their art, creating a ripple effect in the industry. Their collaborative nature, as seen in performances with juniors and other labels' groups, embodies a spirit of unity in K-pop. By mentoring rising stars and sharing insights into the self-production model, they have become role models for aspiring idols.

And on top of all that, Seventeen's approach to teamwork and individual growth has redefined what it means to be a group. Balancing 13 members across vocal, performance, and hip-hop units while maintaining cohesion is a feat that underscores their strong bond. It's a dynamic which is encouraging other up and coming groups to explore unique formations and value individuality within the collective.

The group's foray into diverse media, including variety shows and fashion collaborations, has also broadened their reach. By embracing these opportunities, they have set a precedent for idols to expand their horizons beyond traditional K-pop activities, further elevating the genre's global appeal.

Speaking to the BBC ahead of their Glastonbury appearance in 2024, group leader S. Coups said 'We'd like to reach fans in as many countries as possible because we don't really get to see them that often in person. I still believe that we have a long way to go and we want to become even more successful.'

Their ability to reinvent themselves while staying true to their core identity all points to a continuing bright future. Speculation about potential solo projects, international collaborations, and innovative concepts fuels anticipation among fans and industry insiders alike.

Their expansive discography - ranging from heartfelt ballads like "Don't Wanna Cry" to high-energy hits like "Hot" - also demonstrates their versatility, ensuring their relevance and staying power through various shifts in music trends.

That's not to say that they don't have several challenges ahead. K-pop groups have a huge issue around their longevity, which comes from the South Korean requirement that men aged between 18 and 28 years old enlist in the military for anything between 18 to 21 months depending on which branch of the military they join.

Temporary delays and full or partial exemptions are sometimes granted. Due to their influence and contributions to cultural diplomacy, high-profile figures like K- Pop idols can request deferrals, often receiving permission to postpone enlistment until the age of 30.

Recent changes to regulations, sparked by cases like BTS member Jin's enlistment, clarified age limits for cultural figures. However, they are still expected to fulfil their military duties unless granted exemption.

It's a difficult area to negotiate. Already Jeonghan is away completing his compulsory service and other members are due to enlist during 2025.

The other huge issue in society at the moment, artificial intelligence (AI) is also impacting on music. When Woozi mentioned to reporters that he was interested in the possibilities AI offered it caused a massive media storm. But he didn't mean he was using it for song composition and had to revisit the topic to confirm that all of Seventeen's music is 'written and composed by human creators'.

Seventeen perform on stage during the 8th Gaon Chart K-Pop Awards on January 23, 2019 in Seoul, South Korea

Members of Seventeen live on stage during day 2 of Lollapalooza 2024 at Olympic Stadium in Berlin, Germany, 2024

Of course the group is innovative so its idols were bound to check out AI possibilities – but this was more around creating videos and special effects.

The issue blew up when Woozi told reporters at the launch press conference in Seoul, South Korea, for Seventeen's album and single "Maestro", that the song's music video includes an AI-generated scene and Woozi said that he was 'experimenting' with AI.

'We practised making songs with AI, as we want to develop along with technology rather than complain about it', he said. 'This is a technological development that we have to leverage, not just be dissatisfied with. I practised using AI and tried to look for the pros and cons.'

After the coverage, Woozi took to Instagram to confirm that he and the group have not used the technology in any of their music.

Despite the challenges, Seventeen's journey continues with pace. Their past has laid a foundation of excellence, their present shines with influence, and their future brims with possibilities. In the ever-changing realm of K-pop, Seventeen stands as a timeless symbol of artistry, unity, and the enduring impact of music.

Woozi poses for a photo during a showcase for the group's new compilation album, *17 Is Right Here* in Seoul, April 2024

Discography

EPs (mini albums)

17 Carat May 2015

Boys Be September 2015

Going Seventeen December 2016

Al1 May 2017

You Make My Day July 2018

You Made My Dawn January 2019

Heng:garae June 2020

; [Semicolon] October 2020

Your Choice June 2021

Attacca October 2021

FML April 2023

Seventeenth Heaven October 2023

Spill the Feels October 2024

Seventeen holds a showcase for their third mini album *Going Seventeen* in Seoul, Korea, 2016

Seventeen perform during a showcase for their third mini album *An Ode* in Seoul, September 2019

Seventeen attends *17 Is Right Here* Press Conference at Conrad Seoul in Yeongdeungpo-gu on April 29, 2024 in Seoul, South Korea

7

T HERE

Albums

Love&Letter April 2016

Teen, Age November 2017
+ Director's cut with four new songs in Feb 2018 (Thinkin' about you, Thanks, Run to You and Falling For U).

An Ode September 2019

Face the Sun May 2022

Sector 17 [repackaged Face the Sun] 2022

17 Is Right Here April 2024

Happy Burstday May 2025

Singles

2015

Shining Diamond

Adore U

Mansae

2016

Pretty U

Very Nice

Boomboom

2017

Don't Wanna Cry

Clap

2018

Thanks

Oh MY!

2019

Getting Closer

Home

HIT [First digital single]

Fear

DK of Seventeen takes the stage at BMO Stadium in Los Angeles, California, on November 9, 2024

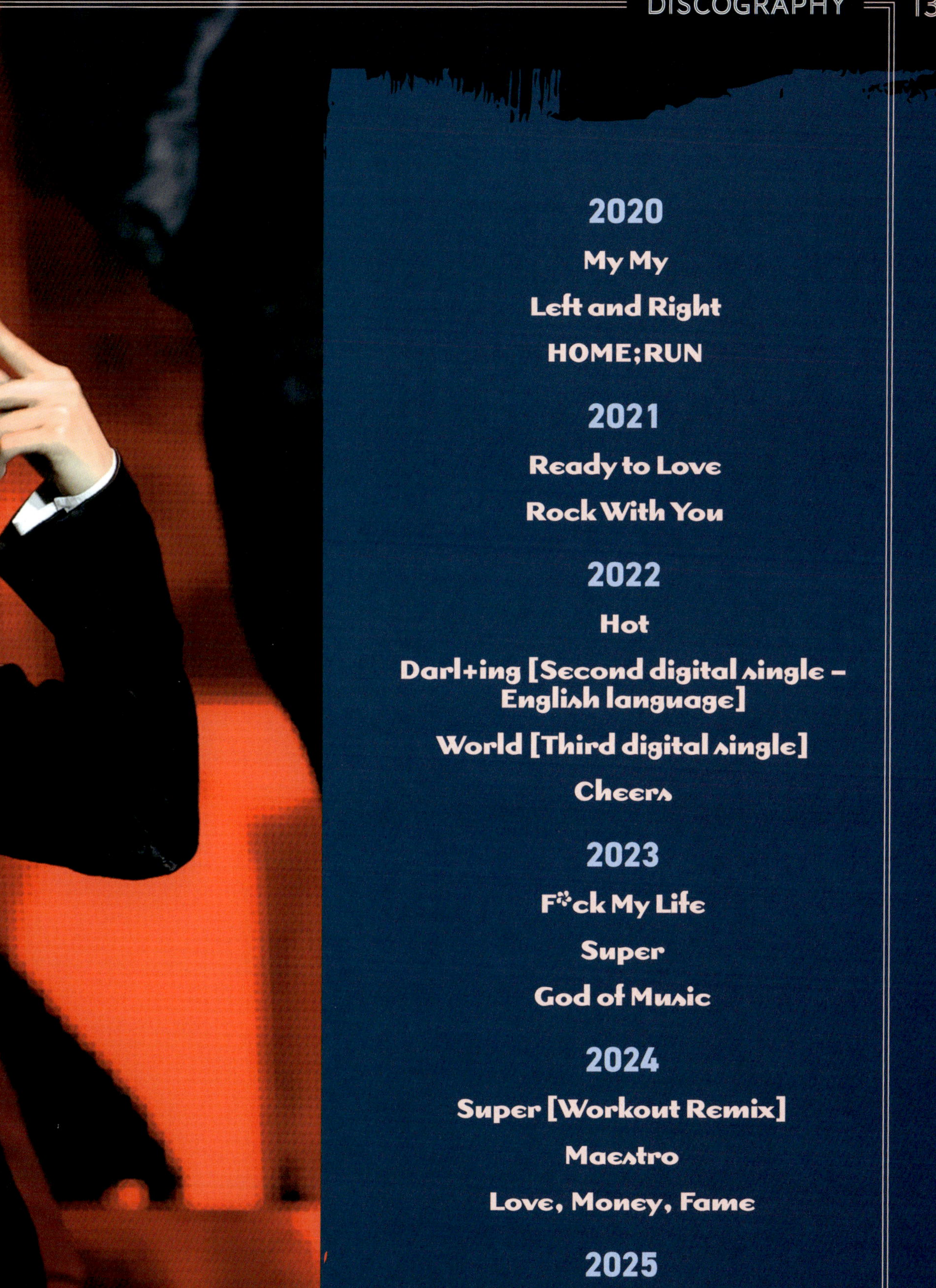

2020

My My

Left and Right

HOME;RUN

2021

Ready to Love

Rock With You

2022

Hot

Darl+ing [Second digital single – English language]

World [Third digital single]

Cheers

2023

F*ck My Life

Super

God of Music

2024

Super [Workout Remix]

Maestro

Love, Money, Fame

2025

Bad Influence

Thunder

Japanese language releases

We Make You mini album* May 2018

Happy Ending single album** May 2019

Fallin' Flower single album April 2020

24H mini-album September 2020

Not Alone single album April 2021

Power of Love special single December 2021

Dream EP, November 2022

Always Yours compilation album, 2023

Shohikigen single November 2024

* Mini-album -A short album with a cohesive theme (typically 4-7 songs total)

** Single album - 1 main song + bonus tracks (smaller release, usually 2-3 songs total)

Seungkwan performs at the 39th Golden Disc Awards at Mizuho PayPay Dome in Fukuoka, Japan, on January 5, 2025

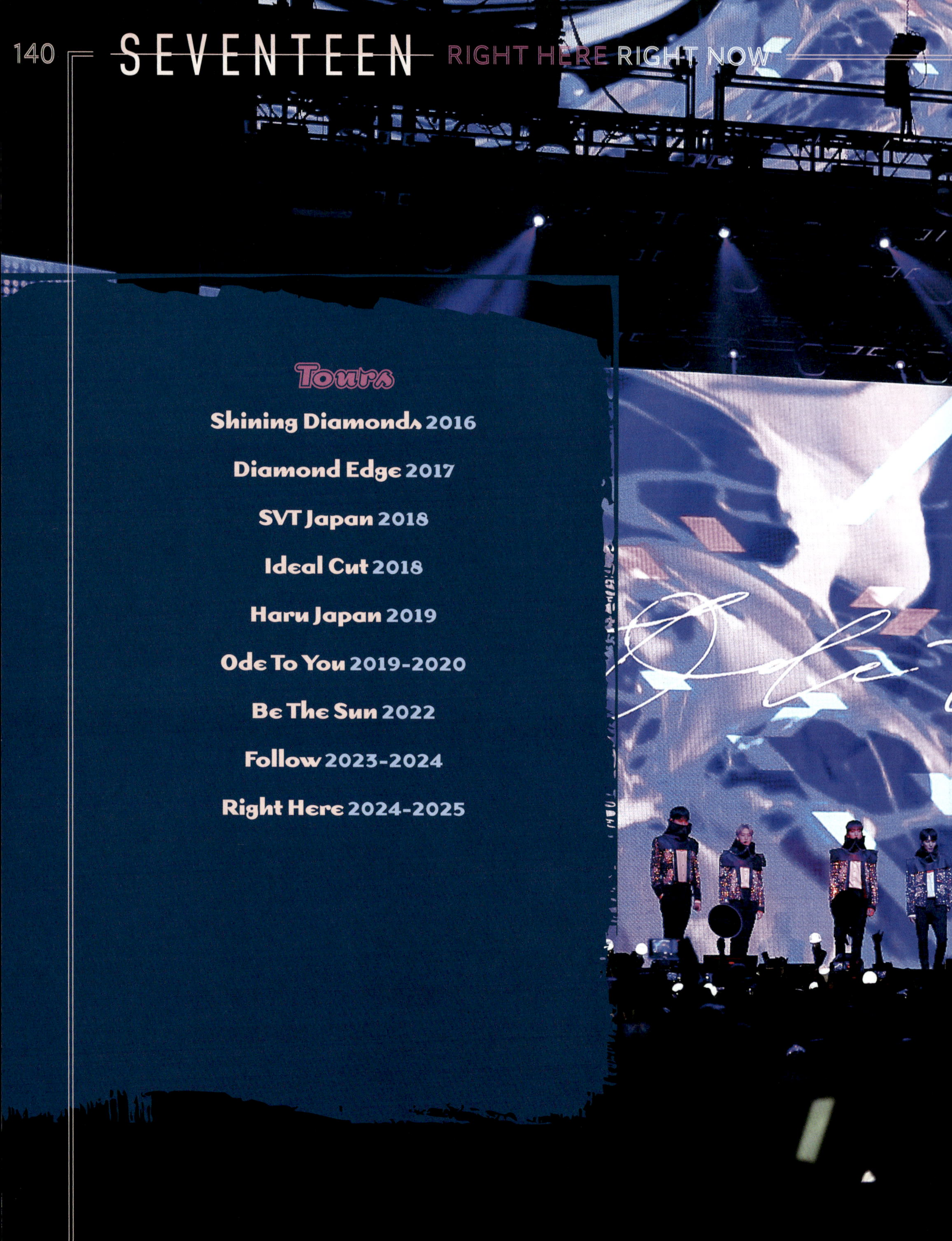

Tours

Shining Diamonds 2016

Diamond Edge 2017

SVT Japan 2018

Ideal Cut 2018

Haru Japan 2019

Ode To You 2019-2020

Be The Sun 2022

Follow 2023-2024

Right Here 2024-2025

Seventeen perform in concert during their Ode to You tour at Toyota Music Factory in Irving, Texas, 2020